PENGUIN BOOKS
THE KISS OF LIFE

EMRAAN HASHMI is a popular Bollywood actor. He shot to fame with his first runaway hit, *Murder*, and since then there has been no looking back.

In 2014, Emraan and his wife, Parveen, were tested like never before. Their four-year-old son, Ayaan, was diagnosed with cancer. Through this book, Emraan recounts his rise to stardom, his son's ailment, his transformation as a human being, and everything in between.

You can follow Emraan through his Twitter handle @emraanhashmi.

BILAL SIDDIQI'S debut novel, *The Bard of Blood*, is a fictional thriller set in Baluchistan. His main interests are writing novels and screenplays, but the topic of this book struck a chord with him. Bilal currently works at Red Chillies Entertainment. He is twenty-one years of age and lives in Mumbai.

You can follow Bilal through his Twitter handle @BilalS158.

EMRAAN HASHMI

with BILAL SIDDIQI

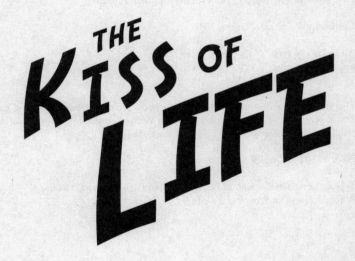

THE KISS OF LIFE

Foreword by Akshay Kumar

BLUE
SALT

PENGUIN BOOKS

PENGUIN BOOKS
Published by the Penguin Group
Penguin Books India Pvt. Ltd, 7th Floor, Infinity Tower C, DLF Cyber City,
Gurgaon 122 002, Haryana, India
Penguin Group (USA) Inc., 375 Hudson Street, New York, New York 10014, USA
Penguin Group (Canada), 90 Eglinton Avenue East, Suite 700, Toronto,
Ontario, M4P 2Y3, Canada
Penguin Books Ltd, 80 Strand, London WC2R 0RL, England
Penguin Ireland, 25 St Stephen's Green, Dublin 2, Ireland (a division of
Penguin Books Ltd)
Penguin Group (Australia), 707 Collins Street, Melbourne, Victoria 3008, Australia
Penguin Group (NZ), 67 Apollo Drive, Rosedale, Auckland 0632, New Zealand
Penguin Books (South Africa) (Pty) Ltd, Block D, Rosebank Office Park,
181 Jan Smuts Avenue, Parktown North, Johannesburg 2193, South Africa

Penguin Books Ltd, Registered Offices: 80 Strand, London WC2R 0RL, England

First published by Penguin Books India and Blue Salt 2016

ISBN 9780143426509

Typeset in Adobe Garamond Pro by Manipal Digital Systems, Manipal
Printed at Replika Press Pvt. Ltd, India

A PENGUIN RANDOM HOUSE COMPANY

To my son, my superhero—Ayaan. Learning from your confidence, courage and resilience, I have grown as a person.
Mamaji and Choti aunty, the two pillars of my life. You both might have gone but your memory will live on in our hearts and minds forever.
I also dedicate this to all the cancer patients who are battling the disease. My family and I offer you our prayers.

A piece of advice from us—hope and the will to survive will get you through every adversity.

CONTENTS

FOREWORD

Cancer! The word every household fears the most. The disease no one deserves. The 'Big C', or, in my eyes, the Cloud that comes, but never passes. It just hovers over you for the rest of your life, silently waiting in the shadows.

I lost my father fifteen years ago to prostate cancer and I blame our own ignorance, as much as fate, for this tragedy.

Did I know then that men should go for an annual PSA (Prostate-Specific Antigen) Test, especially after the age of forty-five? I knew nothing.

Which is why I hope this book aids in spreading awareness. It is awareness that will help us fight this Cloud, it is awareness that can save lives.

Cancer does not only prey on the old and weak, it swoops and takes away people of all ages—people who are precious to you.

When I heard of Ayaan's diagnosis, I felt as if I had been punched in the stomach.

I remember I was driving at that time. I pulled over, found Emraan's number and called him immediately because I know what it's like to have someone you love deeply fall prey to this disease.

It is heart-wrenching to lose a parent, but at least you can console yourself that they have seen places, things, felt love, hope and wonder. But for a parent to see their child undergo the trauma of this disease, their little one who still climbs into their bed in the middle of the night, who comes up to their knees and looks up at them like they are the knight who will slay all his dragons, how do you let him go, let him down? How do you tell him that you have failed in your primary duty as a father—to protect him as long as you live?

I am a father myself and when I imagined walking in Emraan's shoes, my heart sank. I got hold of all my contacts in Canada, the hospital I contribute to, the specialists that I had come across during my own journey, holding my father's hand, fighting this disease. I wanted to do all I could for the man who had just had the rug of life pulled from under him.

I did what I could and Emraan did what every father should do. He fought the battle not only with his son, but he fought it for him as well. Cancer is the hardest on family members. My father suffered for two years before he died, but my family has been suffering for seventeen years, having to live with the regret that we didn't find out sooner.

All I can do is pray that more people become aware and do what they can, as soon as they can.

There are two important lessons that I learned from my family's experience with this terrible disease. One is to know your body, screen irregular things that you notice and take precautions. And the other is to acknowledge the fleeting nature of life.

We are under the illusion that we and our loved ones are going to live forever. That is something that we need to change. Spend time with the people you love; put away your work to play hide-and-seek with your children; sit with your grandparents and listen to their stories of 'Hamare zamane mein . . .'; turn off the TV; lose your phone; and just live and learn and laugh.

Because, we all come with expiry dates. The only difference between us and those milk bottles you see on supermarket shelves is that their 'Best Before' is printed on their lids and ours is flying in the wind.

Love and prayers to all those people, and their families, who have suffered due to this terrible disease. You are braver than you think, and stronger than you feel. You are all heroes!

Akshay Kumar

ONE

'I'M BATMAN!'

'Who is this?'
   I waited for a split second before answering him. I
needed to make sure I replied to him in the right voice. He might
be young, but he's very sharp.

'I'm Batman,' I replied in a low, gruff tone. 'Is that Ayaan?'

There was a pause. I could imagine his eyes widen with
disbelief.

'Y-yes? Is that really . . . *Batman?*'

'How are you, Ayaan?'

'I'm okay, Batman. Are you fighting crime in Gotham? Papa
told me!'

A lump formed in my throat. I decided to tell him what I had
called him for in the first place.

'Would you like to become a superhero like me, Ayaan?'

He breathed heavily with excitement. I could hear it over the
phone.

'Yes!'

'Then listen to me very carefully. It will take some time, but
once we are done, you are going to become better than Iron Man!
You will be Ayaan Man!'

I knew Ayaan loved Batman. But I had already donned that
cape. If I had offered him the chance to be Batman, he wouldn't

have quite liked the idea of us playing the same superhero. The incongruity would get to him. That's how I decided we'll pronounce his name in a way that resembled another one of his absolute favourites—Iron Man.

'Okay,' he replied. 'What will I have to do?'

'Listen to me very carefully, Ayaan . . .'

~

Five minutes later when I walked into the room, I saw him playing with his superhero figurines on the bed. He looked up at me sheepishly. I looked back at him and raised an eyebrow. He was brimming over with excitement, fighting the urge to tell me what had just happened.

'Daddy, guess who called!'

I sat beside him hurriedly, playing along.

'Who?' I whispered, looking at his big, brown eyes attentively.

'Batman,' he grinned. 'He told me how to become a superhero!'

I gasped exaggeratedly, matching his level of excitement, then leaned forward and hugged him tight. My son was going to be a superhero.

~

A light shower fell on the bustling streets of Mumbai as I leaned against a wall in the grim-looking corridor. A drizzle in January was quite uncommon, but it was that kind of day—a morose afternoon, that we conjure up in films so well, often accompanying it with a soft, soulful background track. But this was no film. It was reality. My eyes looked out of the window tracing the distant splash of rain on the helpless commuters. I felt lonely and isolated from them. Their lives seemed so much better than mine. Here I was, at the Hinduja Hospital in Mahim, surrounded by my family. Everything would be okay, they kept telling me. I wanted to believe them. It was 14 January 2014—the beginning of an unexpected journey.

As I heard the creak of the little stretcher that wheeled Ayaan towards the operating theatre, my grip around Parveen's wrist tightened. She followed Ayaan into the freezing air-conditioned room with whitewashed walls, with me in tow. It was the kind of clinical environment I detested. The smell of disinfectant took me back to the days my grandmother was battling for her life in the Intensive Care Unit, not too long ago. I looked at all my family members—my mother, my cousin Smiley Suri, Kumkum Saigal who I refer to as 'Chotumasi', my childhood buddy Sharan— waiting outside. They anxiously nodded in support before we stepped in. The doctors were going to operate upon him. We looked at our little baby, sedated, completely unaware of the grave battle that he was about to fight.

The staff had removed his favourite Batman T-shirt and replaced it with a small green hospital gown. I kissed his forehead gently and placed a *taveez*, an amulet, around his neck.

'Sorry sir,' one of the nurses addressed me as I did this. 'It's a sterile environment. You'll have to remove it.'

I did as I was told and clutched the amulet tightly in my hand. Parveen gave him a tight hug, before we stepped out of the room. As if on cue, my phone vibrated. It was Mahesh Bhatt, my uncle.

'Y—yes Bhatt Sahaab,' I said meekly. Bhatt Sahaab has a way of sensing things; that's probably why he called me at the right time to say what I needed to hear.

'Emmi, Emmi,' he said. 'I'm telling you again. He's going to be fine.'

There was a long pause. I could still not speak.

His voice boomed again: 'Emmi, he's going to be fine!'

It was then that I couldn't hold back. Before I realized it, tears began streaming down my face. I have always been someone who shies away from showing my true emotions, especially during moments when I am vulnerable. But, I had never felt this helpless in my life.

I remembered the night before, when we had tricked Ayaan into believing that we had checked into a hotel. I had met the doctors and nurses in an adjoining room so that he didn't overhear my conversation with them. Once I was back to his room, he threw a fit when he was given the insipid hospital food. He demanded pizza and all the other junk that got him happy. It took us some time to get him to settle down, after which he asked me a simple question.

'Is it my birthday or is it Christmas, Papa?' he enquired earnestly. 'Is that why we are in a hotel? To celebrate?'

'Yes, Ayaan,' I replied. 'It's gonna be your birthday soon and we will celebrate many many more birthdays together!'

My four-year-old baby boy was diagnosed with second-stage Wilms' tumour, a type of cancer that affects the kidneys and typically occurs in children. Wilms' tumour is very uncommon. Children of African origin are relatively more prone to suffer from it than other children. It is named after a German doctor, Max Wilms, who wrote one of the first medical articles about the disease in 1899—it would seem unfortunate for a man to have a damned disease named after him. Because at that moment, I disliked the word itself.

I shuffled nervously, transferring my weight from one foot to the other, waiting to find out what would happen next. I looked at my wife standing beside me. Parveen was composed and certainly more in control than I was. She is a strong woman. Although it was all a façade, but it required more than mere bravery to look that stoic. My forehead on the other hand was creased with anxiety. My heart thumped away so loudly that I feared it would resound in a tormented echo. Here I was, Emraan Hashmi, the actor known to wear different masks for a living, fighting to keep a straight face. But given the turmoil that had hit our lives in the past few days, it was justified. No parent should ever have to see their child suffer. Certainly not with cancer. But fate had played its cards with Ayaan.

I walked around, my shoulders heavy with the weight of helplessness. I didn't utter a word to my family who waited outside. I wasn't in the mood to speak to anyone. *Just let me be for now,* I thought to myself. And they did. They were too tongue-tied, too shaken up to speak themselves. I pulled out my phone and unlocked the screen mindlessly, more out of habit than anything else. On opening the WhatsApp messenger, I noticed that all my friends and loved ones had changed their profile photos to the same picture that I had put up. It was an image from a Batman film, where the Bat symbol is projected from a skyscraper onto the night sky. Everyone had heard of the story that I had concocted for Ayaan, about transforming into a superhero, and changing the display picture was their way of expressing solidarity. I was deeply moved by this simple gesture. I saw a few more texts from people expressing their sadness and pledging support. I was touched and replied to each of them, lest I forget later. And then I saw a text from a prominent producer. I was scheduled to shoot for his film. He had, without consulting me, cancelled shoots indefinitely even though it would cost him and the production house a lot of money. This had my head spinning again. My professional life seemed uncertain but that was the least of my concerns at this moment. However, could I ignore that part of my life for too long? I locked my phone and slipped it back into my pocket, making a mental note to respond to him later when he would come to visit.

Wanting to be alone while the operation was in progress, I went up to the eighth floor of the hospital to sit in the room that we had reserved for Ayaan the night before. It was a hospital suite that overlooked the sea. I stared at the gushing waves with the amulet still clutched in my palm and prayed like I had never prayed before. It was two in the afternoon and the operation was going to go on for another couple of hours.

Dr Uma Ali, who I fondly referred to as Uma aunty, was a family friend. She had tutored a lot of the staff at the hospital and they looked up to her. She gave me hourly updates about the progress and vitals of the surgery from the ICU and that helped me get through the four agonizing hours.

'We are going to get through this,' my wife said as she sat beside me, a tinge of worry showing in her eyes finally. 'It might be a long road ahead, but we will.'

Burying my head in my hands, all the possibilities, especially the bad ones, crossed my mind. *Why him? God, why Ayaan?* I had personally known people who had battled cancer before. I had sympathized with them, but never quite grasped the abysmal pain that the dreaded disease brought with it. Shamin Desai, an incredible human being and friend, had succumbed to stomach cancer while I was shooting with him (his directorial debut, *Raftaar 24x7* was completed by his wonderful wife, Priyanka, who wanted to realize his dream; the movie was retitled *Rush*). Anurag Basu, another friend, with whom I had done two of my biggest hits—*Murder* and *Gangster*—had successfully battled leukaemia. *Two different cases. Two different outcomes.*

I tried to wipe out all negativity from my head. I was successful for a moment. I savoured those few blank seconds. But then it all came back. The calm before the storm. And I realized that I was going to live that nightmarish moment again, for the hundredth time.

~

'Mr Hashmi,' Dr Ravi Ramadwar, the kidney surgeon, called me up around forty minutes post the operation, at around 5 p.m.

'You can come down to the second level. We'll show you the tumour.'

I looked at my family and friends, who had joined me in the room by now. They stared back at me in anticipation.

'The doctor wants to show us the tumour,' I said, with a mixed sense of relief and nervousness. 'I'm going down to the second level. Do you want to come see it too?'

They nodded and stood up, heading towards the lift. I was hoping that in some miraculous way, they were able to save Ayaan's kidney. I walked past the operation theatre. Ayaan was going to be shifted to another room in the recovery section soon. I would find out more once I was done having a quick look at the tumour, *the monster that had been growing inside him.*

The doctor had told us that the surgery was successful and there was no need to worry. I still wore a harrowed expression, as we waited by the lift, hoping that the kidney had been saved. My family looked on at me helplessly. Nothing they could say or do could make me feel better. The lift doors opened after a brief ring.

We stepped in. I pushed the button for the second floor. It took us a few seconds to get there. The doors of the lift opened and we rushed into the corridor. I asked one of the ward boys where Dr Ravi Ramadwar was operating. He looked at me blankly for a while and then broke into a grin.

'Sir, can I have your autograph?'

I was taken aback. He quickly fumbled for a small notepad in his pocket and along with a pen thrust it upon me. I obliged.

'Sir, your film *Gangster* is my favourite! Are you really Emraan Hashmi?'

This wasn't what I wanted at the moment. I just turned around and walked through a door that I thought was the Out Patient Department. Once I stepped in, my eyes met those of a boy, just about old enough to work, clad in white, holding a surgical tray. I could literally hear my heartbeat as he looked at us and nodded. I walked towards him briskly, with my family behind me. I wanted to see the dreaded tumour that had turned our world upside down. As I drew closer, I was stunned . . .

What lay in the tray looked oddly unusual. It was reddish brown, bloody and larger than I had expected. Almost fifteen centimetres long. I was appalled. The doctor had not said that it was this big . . . It looked more like Ayaan's stomach! There had to be something wrong.

'T—tumour? Is that the tumour?'

The boy shot me a confused glance as he held the tray straight out at me to examine that godawful thing.

'Is this the tumour? What the hell is this?'

'That's a damn liver,' my friend Sharan interjected. 'It's not the tumour, Emmi!'

'Yes sir,' the boy exclaimed. 'This is the liver I've been asked to show Mr Mehta's family!'

My eyes almost flew out of their sockets. The rest of my family was aghast too.

'Do I look like Mr Mehta?' I said through gritted teeth.

'There's no tumour here, sir. I'm afraid you've come to the wrong section of the building. The OPD you are looking for is on the other side. It's a common mistake.'

He proceeded to tell us how we could get to where we needed to be. As we walked towards the right OPD, we shot each other quick glances and then cracked up. It was a much needed dose of comic relief. The kind that Shakespeare used in his tragedies, to ease the tension, even if it was only for a few moments.

Finally, we reached the correct OPD, forgetting the comedy of errors we had just witnessed. This time, we were led into a room, where we met the doctor. On a plain white tray, I saw what was the most frightening sight I have ever witnessed. There it lay, the size of a tennis ball. I tasted bile. It wasn't something I could look at for too long. I turned my head away as the rest of my family gasped collectively in shock. The doctor went on to give me both, the good and bad news.

'The good news is, the operation was a success and the tumour was cut out without any spillage. The bad news is, we couldn't save the kidney.'

Ayaan was a brave boy indeed. I have grown to believe that children have a special strength to deal and cope with things. They don't get bogged down by the notions and fears of illnesses. As adults, we are always preoccupied with the baggage we carry and are afraid of our burdens, of illnesses, of death . . . But kids don't have that kind of a problem. Ignorance, as they say, is bliss. I was amazed to see that Ayaan had had that thing growing inside him and had been dealing with it with a cheerful disposition. I was glad that it was out. But everything wasn't over yet. A dagger still dangled over our heads.

The four years prior to this had been a dream run, both professionally and personally. I was truly happy and content. Probably even a little laid-back. But these were testing times. It was a long road ahead, full of challenges and complications. I was not going to let the disease destroy everything that I had built. It was time to get into battle mode, not just for my sake but also for Ayaan. It would take a superhero to walk this path and come out unscathed . . . Could Ayaan be that superhero? Only time would tell.

TWO

THE FORTY-FIFTH TAKE

'Cut! Cut! Cut!'
I looked down at my feet. I could feel the piercing gaze of everyone on the set. I had gone wrong again. *For the twenty-ninth time . . .*

The first wide shot, that is, my first ever shot for a film was fine. I just had to walk into the frame. Sweets were distributed on the set to celebrate the occasion. Then came the time for the close-up, the dialogue shot. That is when I started feeling the pressure, with almost a hundred people staring at me. The performance anxiety was getting to me. Everything that I had learnt in acting class had evaporated into thin air.

'That's all right, Emraan. We're getting there. The atmosphere is probably getting to you. It happens,' Vikram Bhatt, the director, said, masking his exasperation with a calm voice which must have required some effort. He had walked up to me and rested his hand on my shoulder. We have known each other since a long time, so there's great understanding between us. But I knew I had to get my act together soon, before Vikram lost his patience altogether.

'Be a little more emphatic when you say the line. Come on, let's do this.'

As sweat trickled down my forehead, a make-up man quickly scurried up to me with the powder puff and wiped it away. He reapplied the foundation, pressing the puff a bit too hard against my already adequately bronzed face. Even he had had enough.

This was my moment, I thought. I had mentally prepared myself to be an actor. A proper career option. I had been training to do this for the last ten months. And so far, as the night progressed, I felt I was losing every shred of self-confidence I had held within me.

'And . . . ACTION!'

I steadied myself, as the lights brightened on my face. Finding my voice again, I started.

'Batti bandh kar! Battery down ho jayegi to dhakka marne waala yahaan ayega . . . nahi!'

'CUT! Emraan, you paused unnecessarily at the end! It had to be continuous!'

I nodded, realizing I had messed up yet again. I looked at Vikram's pale, tired face, as he took off his specs and rubbed his face vigorously with his free hand. His white hair was ruffled. The entire crew shared his exasperation. Initially they had been encouraging, but now they made no bones about their irritation. I even caught a fleeting smirk on the spot boy's face.

From the corner of my eye, I dared to look at my uncle—Mahesh Bhatt, a prolific film-maker known for his quirks and eccentricities. Just at an arm's length from him sat Bhatt Sahaab's aunt and my grandmother—Purnima Varma, a veteran actress of over a hundred films. And here I was, struggling to deliver a simple, silly line. I had mustered the courage to look at Bhatt Sahaab when he stood up with a flourish after a few seconds of eye contact, slammed shut the book he was reading and stormed off the set erected at Mukesh Mills, Mumbai. As I had always known, there are no half-measures with Bhatt Sahaab. He was angry and the world needed to know.

'Come on, Emmi . . . You're almost there. Let's get rolling.'

Another take. Another failed attempt. Take thirty and everyone had given up. Including my spirit. I was a bundle of nerves. Raw, misplaced energy. Trying too hard, which showed in the footage. Or sometimes, nothing showed.

'We'll try again tomorrow,' Vikram said finally, at his wit's end. He glanced at his watch. It was well past midnight. I walked back to the make-up van for a dinner break. I remember thinking to myself—man, in these ten months I have literally rewired my mind into believing that acting is my calling. What will all my friends say? What would my detractors think? We told you so . . . *'Bada actor banne chala!'* I couldn't help but feel the general disgruntled vibe that engulfed me. The one I had created. It was my first dialogue and second shot in my debut film, *Footpath*, that we were shooting in 2003, and things couldn't have gone worse.

I finally shot a glance at my grandmother, who unlike her nephew had waited patiently to watch her grandson shred the hopes she had pinned on him of becoming an actor. She looked mortified. Maybe she realized that I wasn't cut out to be an actor after all.

~

I was born into a filmy family, so to speak. While for some it would've been an exciting prospect, a stepping stone into Bollywood, if one chose it as a career, I was indifferent. I was open to other options, not being much of a Bollywood buff while growing up. In fact, I had never cared much about Hindi films. If I had the option to pick, I'd choose a Hollywood or foreign language film ten times out of ten. Yes, my upbringing was perhaps Westernized in that sense.

My life was limited to the confines of the suburban village of Bandra in Mumbai. Just as one who has been brought up in Bandra, I stayed in my comfort zone until my college days. I lived a happy, carefree life with my parents Anwar and Maherah

Hashmi, my grandmother and grandaunt in our Pali Hill flat. Pali Hill is a posh, sophisticated part of Bandra. Or as Bhatt Sahaab puts it, the 'Beverley Hills of Mumbai'.

I was a student of Maneckji Cooper, a school in Juhu, in a posh locality by the famous Juhu Beach, a few kilometres from Bandra. After my schooling years, I joined Sydenham College to study commerce. This is where some of the trouble started. I was extremely mischievous and not inclined towards academics—I used to scoff at the idea of studying commerce and the very thought of dealing with numbers put me off. I would scrape through those years somehow, just about managing to pass so that I did not have to retake exams, whiling away my time chasing girls, staying out late at parties, and so on. Being that way had become a lifestyle for me.

I remember one morning, at around five, I had woken up to an alarm that I had set the previous night. My exams were approaching in a few days and with great resolve I had promised myself that I'd wake up early to study and mug up the stuff in my textbooks. I stepped out of my room to get myself a bottle of water when I saw Mukesh Bhattji in our living area, chatting with my grandmother. Mukeshji used to come to our home at five in the morning and ring the bell furiously almost thirty times till somebody opened the door! My grandmother who used to be up at the crack of dawn would let him in yelling Hindi expletives, only to be pampering him moments later. It wasn't uncommon, for she loved chatting with people well into the wee hours of the morning.

Mukeshji looked at my dishevelled state questioningly. He knew about my carefree lifestyle and did not quite approve of it. He, just like Bhatt Sahaab, was a passionate film-maker. And here I stood in my pyjamas, scratching my scruffy nape, fighting to keep my eyes open even while standing. I greeted him and walked into the kitchen, feeling his gaze bore two holes into my back.

'Send him over to the office,' I overheard him tell my grandmother. 'He shouldn't be loafing around.'

My grandmother agreed readily. She probably realized that this was one way to get me into the film world. Me? I just shrugged and thought about the exam at hand. I was staring down the barrel of the dreaded shotgun every college kid knows as 'examinations'; I would dodge one bullet at a time.

The next morning my grandmother asked me what I planned to do in the future in a nonchalant, by-the-way tone. She secretly hoped I would want to be an actor too. Not many people know this, but before acting in feature films, I had done around fifteen advertising campaigns as a kid with brands like Rasna, Bournvita, Good Knight, Gems and a few others. I did my first ad for Good Knight mosquito repellent and was paid two thousand five hundred rupees. That was my first salary, at the age of four! My last ad was a disaster though. It was for Cadbury Gems and I had to pop out from behind a sofa and mouth a dialogue. I began to feel very exposed for some reason and began to cry. I was eight years old and was probably beginning to go through social and emotional changes. I started feeling judged for the first time. I didn't really know if I wanted to face the camera again after that! But my grandmother would keep bringing it up.

'I mean, it's not like you're good at what you're doing right now either,' she chuckled mockingly. 'You don't get good grades, you have no goals or ambitions. What the hell are you planning to do with your life?'

I was horrible with numbers. My grandma, just like Mukeshji, had a point. There was only so much bumming around that I could do. I needed to explore a few avenues to find something interesting for myself. After my exams were over, I spent a serious amount of time wondering what to do next. I still had a semester of college left, and most of my friends had started working or doing internships at various places. I needed to do something too.

Before college, in fact, I had decided to take on a part-time job as a salesman. I hadn't understood the ABC of commerce, even though I had 'studied' it in junior college. It wasn't my cup of tea. But I felt that since I had taken it up, I should give it a fair shot, and what better way than to go out into the field and do some practical stuff, right? There was a job vacancy for a door-to-door salesman and I took it on. I was given fifty rupees a day for food and travel and my wares were hand and shoulder massagers. Sometimes I did manage to sell stuff and sometimes I would have the door slammed on my face! That particular summer I learnt an important lesson in life—keeping one's sense of humour alive is necessary to be able to handle humiliation. It also taught me to be humble and grounded. But by the end of the summer I knew it was not my calling.

I have been an avid gamer right since college and have literally seen video games evolve from the basic Atari to the current ones on Blu-ray discs! I was also a huge fan of Michael Jackson. Just like everyone else around me at that time, I guess. His videos had a certain vision that was ahead of the times. Probably by a generation or two. I remember watching *Thriller* often, extremely fascinated by the make-up, the stunningly realistic visuals. I knew what I wanted to do right then! Nope. It wasn't learning how to dance (which I still need to learn, by the way). Or taking up singing (which I do pretty well on screen now). But it was my penchant for video games that led me to my career choice. Yes, I had enrolled myself for a special effects, VFX and animation class, and was even hoping to follow it up with a trip to the United States for an advanced course in it. But, well, life had other plans and I certainly wasn't going to be a pioneer in the field of VFX!

After having a discussion with Mukeshji, he suggested I drop by at his office. He told me how a film is essentially made at the edit table. Editors are the real heroes of a film, I was told. I toyed with that idea in my head for a bit. With great gusto, I promised him that I'd be at his office right after college. I'd love to be an editor. I absolutely loved the idea. I would be the real hero of the film. I lasted a week.

It was tedious, to say the least. There were a few software I couldn't understand at all. Just looking at them made me nervous. Like my exam paper in financial management. I had another option though. I started assisting Vikram and Bhatt Sahaab on some scripts that were being written for Vishesh Films since about six months. Around that time Vikram Bhatt was shooting a television series called *Dhund* for Bhatt Sahaab's daughter and my cousin, Pooja Bhatt. Riding high on the success of his film *Ghulam* with Aamir Khan and Rani Mukerji, Vikram was certainly someone who was doing it right and had a lot of knowledge to impart. Mohit, my cousin, and I assisted Vikram for *Dhund*.

The shooting for *Dhund* took place at a small bungalow in Pali Hill, Bandra. I was a complete bum on the set. I used to faff around and avoid the odd jobs like setting up the artefacts that needed to be in a frame for a shot, moving around objects, and so on. I remember having to call an actor from his vanity van once the set-up for a shot was ready. I wasn't very comfortable with that job. It was probably the arrogance of a teenager or the contempt I felt for Bollywood itself. I did it once or twice, and that was it. I started playing truant. Observing Mohit and me work around the set Bhatt Sahaab probably realized that Mohit was more cut out for the discipline required of a director than I was.

I made up my mind that I'd start afresh with his next project. That was what I had told Mohit too. A fortnight after the shoot for *Dhund* wrapped up, Vikram had started work on a new film called *Kasoor*. He had finalized the script even while shooting for the TV series and had started work on it soon after. That's how dedicated Vikram was to his work. Mohit and I were going to be formal assistant directors on that project.

Soon we returned on set to work with Vikram. But I didn't really enjoy the experience and the work that came with being an AD. Vikram wasn't someone who'd chase me down or check up on how often I had attended the shoots.

'Man, this is not for me,' I remember telling Mohit one time after college on our way to the sets on the local train. 'I can't be a director.' He on the other hand went on to tell me how he quite enjoyed it and even considered it to be his true calling. That train journey probably underlined our future paths.

Soon after, I stopped going to the shoots altogether. This was yet another job option that I crossed off my list. Direction, it seemed, wasn't for me. And that was the end of that.

'I guess we'll just have to make him an actor,' Bhatt Sahaab had once said on the sets of Vikram's film. He was extremely intuitive and sensed my reluctance while I trudged around lifting objects to set up a frame.

Bhatt Sahaab mentioned it again later on. This time to me in person. I remember refusing. I mean, subconsciously, I always wanted to become an actor. But I didn't know if I had it in me. Bhatt Sahaab provided that much needed nudge in that direction.

'Okay then,' he said and didn't bring it up again that day.

But that night, my grandmother summoned me to the living room. I walked out lazily and stood before her. She gestured me to sit.

'Mahesh tells me that you brushed away the idea of becoming an actor even before he could complete his sentence?'

I opened my mouth to respond, but she cut me short.

'You're a fool, if you did! Do you know how many people out there would give an arm to be presented with such an opportunity?'

I nodded briefly, avoiding her glare.

'You're going to go and speak to him tomorrow itself. I'll have a word with him too.'

The conversation had ended before I could speak. My grandmother and her sister, Pushpa, were rightly called the Mafia by the rest of our family. At that time, she must've been around seventy, but she was as robust and imposing as ever.

'Acting is in your blood,' she added as I walked back towards my room. 'It'll be a pity if you don't give it a shot.'

And so a member of the Mafia had decided my career path.

I used to look into the mirror and know instantly that I was not actor material. The scruffy hair, the shadowy stubble, the distinct eyes. But there had always been an inherent charm, I was told. Something about the vibe that I gave off. Well, why not give it a shot? I mean my grandmother kept insisting. A few others had mentioned it in passing. I had already done a few ad campaigns and had no problem facing a camera as such, even as a kid. I had also assisted Vikram when he was shooting for a few short episodes for an MTV show called *Bheja Fry*. I had to make a short one-minute appearance in that. We all have an idea of how we look, and our self-image is generally a projection of how we see ourselves in our heads. I was no exception. That self-image I had of myself was pretty much shattered in that one minute! I was so self-critical that I couldn't think of bringing myself to act. When I told my grandmother about this, all she said was—'Actors are very harsh on themselves. It is this self-criticism that should challenge you to push yourself harder . . . This comes with time, Emmi. You'll see!'

I remember walking into Room No. 1 in Filmalaya Studios the next day while Vikram was shooting his film. It was a huge make-up room where Bhatt Sahaab relaxed and read scripts and some other books. I greeted him and sat beside him nervously.

He raised an eyebrow at me, as if to say, 'What now?' I bluntly told him about my decision to give acting a shot. He breathed in and looked at the ground.

'I knew it,' he boomed finally. 'I knew you were too lazy to be a director. And I knew you'd come back to me yourself.'

I didn't know whether to smile or to feign an ashamed look. I went with the latter. But there's no fooling Bhatt Sahaab.

'Well, I always knew you had an actor in you,' he grinned mischievously before his face turned serious. 'But it's not an easy job, let me tell you that. We'll see if you can do it, but this is not some damn charity. Get that straight. You don't contribute to the company, we'll throw you out!'

Just then Vikram opened the door and walked in.

'Hey,' he continued, his voice getting louder, finally hitting crescendo, 'This guy wants to be a hero!'

I felt the condescension in his tone. It was probably meant humorously, but it still stung a little. Vikram who had sensed the mocking undertone in Bhatt Sahaab's words was nice enough to ignore it.

Bhatt Sahaab's grin grew wider. 'What do you think?'

'That is good,' Vikram mumbled unconvincingly, barely audible. He shrugged, turned around and left the room as quickly as he had entered it. Bhatt Sahaab laughed.

'Anupam Kher is shooting for his film right now,' Bhatt Sahaab continued. 'He's starting an acting school soon. Go meet him and have a word with him in Room No. 7. Tell him I sent you.'

I looked at Bhatt Sahaab for a few seconds. He was looking at me, the smirk still on his face. I got up and walked out. I had to look for Anupam Kher's room for a while, before I could locate it. A few fans waited outside for an autograph.

There's a common term in Bollywood jargon which I had always heard and found particularly odd. It's 'struggler', used to describe someone who is trying to get a break and become an actor, actress, director, etc. in the film industry. I remember laughing at the term when I had first come across it, but here I was . . . standing outside Anupam Kher's room, like a struggler.

Finally, he walked out of his room and hurried towards his car. I followed him briskly, shoving myself past the enthusiastic fans and managed to tap him on his shoulder until he stopped for a fraction of a second as he opened the door of his car.

'Sir, I am Emraan Hashmi. Mahesh Bhatt has sent me to speak to you, I'm his neph—'

He slammed the door shut and the car took off. It was humiliating and insulting. I returned to Bhatt Sahaab and told him what had just transpired. He was angry that someone treated his nephew that way. He picked up the phone and called Anupam Kher right away.

'I had sent my nephew, Emraan, to speak to you. You cut him off and left!'

There were apologies from the other end. He said he didn't know. He probably would've if he had given me that chance to introduce myself properly. Bhatt Sahaab finally put the phone down.

'I have another friend,' he said finally. 'He'll teach you how to act. He's a veteran, a maestro of theatre and has even written screenplays and acted in films!'

And that's how I met my first guru in the realm of acting, Prithviraj Dubey.

I met Dubeyji at his acting workshop at Prithvi Theatre in Juhu. I remember walking in a few minutes late and finding him seated in a corner of the room. A student was standing, pointing at a wall, reciting something strange. I was confused, as I sat cross-legged beside the other students.

I learned soon enough that the student was reciting a Hindi verse titled 'Manushya ka Aatmabodh'. We were supposed to memorize the whole thing, take our positions, point at a wall and recite it a zillion times. It would help us concentrate, I was told. I did it for about eight sessions and there was still no sign of Dubeyji shifting to another activity. I was exasperated. If this is what becoming an actor was about, I'd rather do something else. I remember complaining about it to Bhatt Sahaab one evening. He was understanding. He called Dubeyji again and told him politely that my film was about to go on the floors soon, and unlike theatre which takes over a year to get rolling, film-making is a more rushed process and he needed to prepare me for it quicker. Dubeyji agreed to teach me privately for a month.

I used to travel to his house which was around half an hour away from mine in Bandra-Kurla Complex. He would always ask me to bring him fruits, which I would lug around until I dropped them on a small table in an otherwise desolate house. There was no sofa, no bed, no nothing. He would sleep on a mat. It was difficult for me, who took the luxuries I had at my disposal for granted, to imagine leading such an ascetic life.

His sessions helped me a great deal. This time round he gave me passages I would understand. I would learn them, then recite them to him. After which he would make me work on my posture, expression, dialogue delivery and voice clarity. It was great fun. After a month of many such sessions, I moved on to Roshan Taneja's acting school.

His was a slightly more filmy way of approaching acting, so to speak. We were given passages from Amitabh Bachchan's films like *Deewar* and other iconic Bollywood monologues. While the other students, around eight in a batch, ended up emulating the actors they had seen on screen, I was fresh in my approach since I had not grown up on these films. I used to just do it my way, without any reference point. That worked for me, because it's very easy for an actor to fall into the trap of copying mannerisms, tones and the general style of another actor. None of that happened with me, luckily.

I was beginning to warm up to the routine and started enjoying my training sessions. But two months into the classes, Bhatt Sahaab learnt that the well-known actor Govinda was pulling out of a film opposite Ameesha Patel (then a rising actress) due to issues with dates. Bhatt Sahaab leapt at the opportunity and simply said to the producer, Mukesh Bhatt, 'Emmi will do the film.'

I was scared out of my wits. I wasn't mentally prepared to star in the film—*Yeh Zindagi Ka Safar*. When I voiced my concerns they decided to conduct a photoshoot with Ameesha and me. The results of that photoshoot were appalling. I looked worried, out of place and downright awkward. Ameesha too told Bhatt Sahaab that I wasn't cut out for it yet. Understandably, she didn't want to work with someone who would drag down a movie, after coming fresh from a super-hit like *Kaho Na Pyaar Hai* with Hrithik Roshan.

'Do you want to do the film, Emmi?' Bhatt Sahaab asked me solemnly. 'We could find another actress who'd be willing to work with you.'

As much as I may have appreciated the thought, it wasn't in my book of ethics to oust someone else just to get a role. I turned him down.

'Besides, I'm not ready yet,' I argued.

'You'll never be ready at this rate!' he exclaimed. 'Not now! Not after six months! You're simply unwilling to get out of your comfort zone.'

I kept quiet. Even though I refused to act in the film I would frequent the sets of *Yeh Zindagi Ka Safar* once it had gone on floors. I was replaced by Jimmy Shergill. I would go and watch Ameesha and Jimmy shoot, and hover around the set to make myself seen. I must admit that it had hurt my ego a bit to see someone else essay a role I was supposed to do.

At that point, Bhatt Sahaab had just started writing a thriller called *Footpath*. It had drugs and cops, and he was assembling all his research material together. He was already done with writing a few scenes and was planning to go with Vikram to Ooty for a schedule of his horror-thriller *Raaz* and finish writing the script. I was hopeful to star in *Footpath*.

'I'm going to Ooty later this week,' he continued. 'I want you to come along. I'll prepare you. Just twenty days.'

Those last three words resonated in my ears. *Just twenty days.* And it wasn't as I had imagined. It was much, much worse.

'Emmi! Stop moving!' Bhatt Sahaab yelled from his bed at 3 a.m. I was lying on an uncomfortable sofa in a suite at the Monarch Hotel in Ooty. A little light leaked from his room into the hall where I was sleeping. There was always a light on in his room. But that was the least of my problems. It was a strange experience staying with him.

I had landed in Ooty the previous day and realized that I had goofed up majorly. While leaving from Mumbai, I was supposed to bring along some research documents pertaining to drugs and some other papers, which were going to help Bhatt Sahaab write the script. I picked them up from the office and headed towards the airport. Whilst getting off, I forgot to take that entire folder of papers with me. That was how irresponsible I was. Bhatt Sahaab was furious and promised himself that he would discipline me.

Living with him was tough for me, to say the least. If indeed there is such a thing as reincarnation, I am pretty sure Bhatt Sahaab was a bat in his previous life. He used to sleep very little. Just an hour or two at most, in a day. He would stay up all night, reading or discussing work on the phone. And if I as much as moved a muscle on the sofa, he would sense it and call out! That was enough to disturb him. He would be writing the script and would be in his zone. When I did fall asleep, he would come and wake me up every day at around four-thirty in the morning by throwing pillows at me. All of this, just so that I could accompany him on a walk down the serene lanes of Ooty. We would never speak a word. He would think about the script, and I would walk along like a zombie, tired and sleep-deprived.

Sometimes, he would urge me to go on the sets of *Raaz* and watch the film being shot. I enjoyed the idea of being an actor, of being in the limelight, as I watched Bipasha Basu and Dino Morea shoot the scenes. My ego had been a little hurt at the fact that someone else thought that I wasn't fit for the earlier chance I had got with *Yeh Zindagi Ka Safar*. But I felt I was a little more prepared for *Footpath* than I was before.

We returned to Mumbai with Bhatt Sahaab having finalized the script. The good thing with him is, as soon as he's made up his mind to shoot a film, everything goes on floors right away without any delay. Same was the case with *Footpath*. It was an interesting premise. Vikram was going to direct it. He offered me the lead role of Arjun Singh. But when I read the script, I read it very differently. I could see myself playing the role of the second lead. It was a character named Raghu. A dark, devilish guy who grows to be a gangster. With Raghu I discovered my penchant for playing grey characters. I told Vikram that I could see myself playing Raghu more convincingly. He mulled over it for a bit. And then, he agreed.

So far everything had gone my way. I had supportive family members who were willing to back me in the best of ways, great gurus, I had a great script at hand, a great director, talented co-stars. Now all I needed to do was to act well. I had failed the test on the first day. The next day was going to be a litmus test of sorts for me. My future and my career depended on it.

~

Take 45. I stood in front of the camera again. *Yesterday was a disaster. I had spent the entire night practising that one dialogue more than a hundred times. Today isn't going to be bad. Today is mine. It's a new evening. New beginnings. I'm going to seize the moment.*

I had learned that Mukeshji had called up Vikram after my disastrous performance the previous day. 'Do you think he's got what it takes to deliver?' he had asked. I had to prove myself.

Vikram was in his chair, leaning forward. He saw me standing on my marker, a lot more confident than I had been yesterday. I looked at him and nodded.

'And . . . ACTION!'

'Batti bandh kar! Battery down ho jayegi to dhakka marne waala yahaan ayega nahi!'

I had delivered the dialogue perfectly. It was a three-page scene—I remember knocking it off in just three takes. There was thunderous applause on the set. After pack-up that night, Praveen Bhatt—the cinematographer of the film—texted Bhatt Sahaab. It was a message that he forwarded to me. It read:

'Congrats, we have a star in the family!'

THREE

WHEN CANCER RAISED ITS UGLY HEAD

January 2014. Parveen, Ayaan and I were on our way back home from a much-needed vacation in Bali. We had a great time welcoming in the New Year. We had revelled away, hoping that the coming year would be fulfilling and better than the last. Personally, it had probably been the most relaxing of holidays I had had in a while. Spending time with each other and letting our hair down on the Indonesian island was refreshing and rejuvenating. But as soon as I boarded the flight back to Mumbai, I started preparing myself for what lay ahead in my professional life.

As I took my seat by the window, I pulled out a diary and a laptop from my bag. I planned to chalk out the schedule for the year, noting down all my professional commitments and figuring out the schedule for the three new films that I had taken on. The three films, *Raja Natwarlal*, *Mr X* and *Hamari Adhuri Kahani* were going to take up some time, and the schedules spilled way into 2015. It was busy times ahead for me, but I knew I could manage it easily if I adhered to the dates. I have always been disciplined with my timing and precise with my schedules. I usually get a broad itinerary in place well in advance. But fate had other plans in store.

It was a few days after we had returned when Parveen came into the room, a tinge of anguish in her expression. She had just bathed Ayaan and her hands were dripping with water.

'It's getting a little more swollen,' she said. 'Come, have a look.'

I got up and followed her to Ayaan's bedroom. He was sitting on his bed, playing with his toys. I sat beside him and hugged him, letting my hand slide under his shirt and on to his belly. He chuckled a bit. I could feel a little more mass on him than usual. I asked him to lie down, and once he complied, I lifted his shirt. His stomach bulged a little. I smiled at Parveen.

'Why's his tummy bulging like that?' I pondered over it for a moment and then just shook my head. 'He's just put on a little weight. That's a good thing.'

Ayaan was very lean, bordering on scrawny. I was in fact a little happy to see some fat on him. I had brushed off Parveen's worries, exactly a month before, in early December 2013, when she had first spotted his stomach coming out a little more than usual. The bulge this time, though, had increased by a fraction. I still wasn't perturbed. The paediatrician we had consulted hadn't found anything alarming during the routine check-up before the Bali trip. If there was something, wouldn't he have brought it to our notice? I shrugged it off and left Ayaan to his toys.

~

As a kid, I was detected with thalassemic tendencies which I carry till date. Thalassemia is a form of an inherited blood disorder, characterized by an abnormal formation of haemoglobin. The abnormal haemoglobin, in turn, results in improper oxygen transport and the destruction of red blood cells. People with thalassemia make less haemoglobin and have fewer circulating red blood cells than normal, which more often than not leads to anaemia. I had realized a short while ago that Ayaan had inherited it from me. It was worrying, but nothing serious, I was assured by everyone I had mentioned it to. People with thalassemia lead a normal life without any serious problems. But I wanted to be doubly sure. Needless to say, I had taken him to a doctor, who prescribed a folic acid tablet. The doctor told me that it would suffice. After our little getaway to Bali, I returned home and purchased the necessary supplements.

It was around eleven in the morning, on the Sunday that followed our return from our vacation and the little panic that Ayaan's tummy had caused Parveen. Ayaan was hobbling around cheerfully, when Parveen brought him the folic acid tablet. He looked at it, shook his head and began to run away from Parveen.

'Wait a second,' I told her. 'Let's crush the tablet first and mix it in water. That'll make it easier for him to swallow.'

She handed me the tablet and a glass of water, and walked towards Ayaan, who was running around playfully. Seeing her come towards him was for him an indication of a chase. I smiled to myself and began to mix the crushed tablet with the water when I heard a dull thud. Ayaan had fallen flat on his face and stomach, after tripping over a rolled-up carpet that the cleaning lady had forgotten to open up. But we didn't rush to help him stand up. In our house, we deliberately don't fuss over minor injuries or falls. We just shrug them off as something that is a part of growing up and learning. It was all a way to prepare him and toughen him up to withstand the brutal world that awaited him.

'Brave boy,' I said smiling at him as he stood up. 'Here, drink this water quickly! And then we're gonna take you out for some pizza!'

He grinned and gulped down the water, forgetting the fall immediately. Four or forty, pizza has that effect on people, I think.

After a couple of hours, we got ready and dressed Ayaan up for a brunch at Taj Land's End, which is situated at Bandstand in Bandra. For us, it's a cosy, convenient place, with a relaxed atmosphere. We took a table facing the sea and eased into our chairs. I wanted to spend as much quality time with the two of them as I could before my hectic shoot schedules got under way.

'Pizza!' Ayaan clapped excitedly as I placed the order. I grinned at him fondly. I loved his smile. It left me weak.

'We need to take him for his vaccination,' Parveen addressed me. 'Let's do it this week?'

Ayaan looked up alert, a tinge of fear in his eyes on hearing the dreaded word which he couldn't even pronounce.

'NO INJECTION!' he spluttered, his eyes already welling up. Parveen realized that she shouldn't have brought it up. But she was just thinking out loud. Luckily, just then the waitress walked in with the pizza and the soft drinks.

'Your pizza's here,' I said. 'Come on, start eating or I'm gonna finish it instead!'

Ayaan grabbed a slice. He had his priorities straight. I, on the other hand, was figuring out how to avoid the injection. There probably had to be another way. If he didn't like it, I didn't want to put him through it. I, for one, hated needles myself. I made a mental note to discuss it with Parveen when he wasn't around.

'I want to use the toilet,' he said as he slurped on his cola. 'Mama, take me! I really need to go!'

Parveen stood up and took him by his hand to the washroom. I decided to answer some phone calls.

She helped him put on his pants very quickly and came rushing towards me in a panicked state.

I still remember the look on Parveen's face when she came back hurriedly from the bathroom, with Ayaan close on her heels. She was pale. Ayaan on the other hand was jovial, as though nothing had happened. I still remember her face, drained of blood, and the words she spoke to me as she took her seat.

'Emmi, you're going to freak out about what I'm going to tell you,' she said. 'I just saw something. I don't know what just happened . . .'

The way she said it made me think she had just witnessed a ghost.

'What are you rambling on about?' I said. 'Go on, tell me!'

And then she did. Her words gave me the chills, thinking about it still does.

'Ayaan just urinated blood.'

My mouth fell open.

'Just like the paints we use in art class, Papa!' Ayaan said, very amusedly.

~

We rushed out of the restaurant, after I settled the bill hastily. Parveen made a series of calls as I drove back home. She called his paediatrician, who insisted that we come to the Hinduja Hospital in Khar without further ado. He was in the Mahim branch of the hospital at that point, and he said he'd rush and see us at Khar instead. We reached home, without having had lunch. My mind was racing and I was hoping that the blood would've been a one-off thing. I was praying hard. We made Ayaan drink a lot of water before we left for the hospital, to see if he passed blood in his urine again. And this time, I saw it too. A stream of blood for an entire fifteen seconds.

To say Parveen and I were worried, would have been an understatement. We rushed Ayaan right away to Dr Ajit Gajendragadkar in Hinduja Hospital, Khar. Ajit was Ayaan's new paediatrician, as we hadn't been too satisfied with the last one. Unfortunately, we hadn't told him about Ayaan's abnormal stomach weight gain earlier.

'What could've caused the bleeding, doctor?'

'I'll run a few tests,' he replied. 'Nothing definitive until then. That's why I'm going to do it right away.'

My father had already accompanied Ayaan into the general ward, a little enclosure separated by a curtain. The doctor stood up after he was informed that they were ready to conduct the tests.

'He had a folic acid tablet for the first time today,' I said quickly, matching steps with the doctor. 'Could that be it?'

'It would be highly unlikely,' he responded. 'Folic acid doesn't do that.'

I couldn't think of anything else, until it hit me.

'He also fell earlier today, flat on his face! He tripped over a carpet . . .'

The doctor walked into the ward and into the enclosure. He turned and looked at me and my wife. She hadn't spoken a word, but I could sense the misery.

'I really can't say until we've run the tests, Mr Hashmi. We'll let you know as soon as we get the results. My guess is that it's an enlarged spleen. When I felt his stomach, there was a swelling on the left side. That could be an indication.'

Parveen and I shot each other a shocked glance.

'An enlarged spleen? But he's so young! Doc—'

'It's a guess,' he said, closing the conversation for now with a reassuring smile. 'We'll let you know soon! I'm pretty sure it's nothing to worry about.'

I looked at my dad and my wife, and then at Ayaan. He was lying down quietly on the spic and span white bed. He wore a puzzled expression. I hated the sight of needles. Just earlier in the day, I was wondering how I'd get Ayaan to avoid routine vaccinations. And now, here he was.

'I'll wait out,' I said to Parveen softly, as the nurse opened a little container for the blood sample. I brushed past the curtain and moved out of the room. I sat down on the chair outside and buried my head in my hands.

'Oh God, where have you brought us,' I sighed. 'From a holiday to a hospital!'

My thoughts were interrupted by a blood-curdling shriek. They had probably just pushed in the needle for the blood sample. Ayaan began to bawl. I couldn't bear him crying. The doctor stepped out. I sprang to my feet, instinctively.

'The blood sample has been taken. We'll be examining his chest and then taking a sonography tomorrow,' he said. 'This might take a while. The results of the blood test, of course, will be given to you tomorrow.'

I slumped back in the chair, rested my head against the wall and closed my eyes. Later that evening, I decided to do some research myself.

The popular search engine—Google—is a most frightening place, I feel. Just like the rest of the Internet is, actually, if you don't know how to filter stuff out. It is both a boon and a bane. It can inform you, as well as sow the seeds of paranoia, all at the behest of a couple of clicks. I learnt that the hard way. Parveen and I crouched over my laptop the same night, around nine, once we had returned from the hospital. I punched in the words 'causes for blood in urine' and hit the search button. We scrolled through several possibilities, noting them down on a pad as we read them. And then we stopped at one, one that made me go numb instantly. A single word—*cancer*. I shuddered.

The nib of Parveen's pen hovered over the paper. She didn't want to write it. I didn't want her to write it either. She just shook her head in the negative.

'Can't be,' she put on a brave tone. 'I mean . . . the doctor . . . would've mentioned it, wouldn't he?'

She is probably right, I thought. But I was sucked into the deadly abyss of paranoia. I am that kind of a person. I slammed the laptop shut. I'd had enough.

'It'll be nothing.' I looked at Parveen. 'It'll be nothing at all. Nothing can happen to him.'

She clutched my hand. We stared at each other, both trying to reassure one another with just our eyes. Ayaan stepped into the room, as if on cue, and looked at us wide-eyed. I motioned him to walk over to us. He did, a little reluctance in his step. Ayaan is great at reading us. He knew something was off. But he came anyway. The three of us joined each other in the tightest of embraces, avoiding his tummy area.

'Okay, Ayaan. It's time to sleep.'

Parveen had found her authoritative tone back. She guided him to his room. There was a new weight on my chest. A lump in my throat. That horrible thought that I just couldn't shake off. *God, please . . . Don't let this be cancer.*

I decided to distract myself. I changed into a pair of track-pants and put on a T-shirt. I headed to the gym. I hopped onto the treadmill, plugged in my earphones and began to run. It didn't do me any good. I increased the speed on the machine. I sprinted at a maddening pace, one that I had never tried earlier. Sweat poured down my face. But the music didn't help. Nor did the running. There was no running away from this thought. *Please don't let this be cancer.*

I have always been one of those people who have a good undisturbed night's sleep. No burden on my conscience to worry me, no problems. No nothing. Parveen had already drifted into a silent sleep. We hadn't talked much after I returned from the gym. Usually, I would be the first one to fall asleep. *But tonight was different . . .* As I tossed and turned restlessly, there was only one thought that ate away at my insides.

Please don't let this be cancer. God, not cancer . . .

But my prayers that night fell on deaf ears.

~

Parveen, Ayaan and I stepped into the Hinduja Hospital at ten minutes to eleven the next day. I had bad memories of the place. My grandmother, Purnima Varma, had succumbed to Alzheimer's and passed away at the very same hospital. That was an additional emotional baggage that I carried as we entered. Flashes of her last moments played through my mind. Coupled with the current thought that had been plaguing my head, I was a toxic mess. But I tried my best to look calm.

We were supposed to do the chest X-ray and the sonography. I remember sitting in the waiting room, as Parveen took Ayaan to get the chest scanned first. In the interim, I ran through the blood test results, which were all normal. That was certainly a relief. After the chest X-ray was conducted, we took him to the sonography room. The doctor in charge applied a cold gel, as Ayaan giggled away because of the tickling sensation. This was all very new for him. The doctor held the ultrasound machine over Ayaan's right side first. No abnormalities. Then, he began to scan his left side. He paused and frowned. He bent over and took a closer look at the screen in front of us. We tried to make something out of it too, but drew a blank.

'What is it, doctor? Did you see something?' I asked. The stony silence at the other end began to worry me.

'Nurse, has Dr Ajit come in yet?' The doctor ignored me and turned towards the nurse instead.

'Yes,' she said. 'He is seeing a patient right now.'

Without another word, he darted out of the room, visibly flustered. The way he had reacted scared Parveen and me. My heart thumped away against my ribcage, and the blood rushed to my head. I sensed something was horribly wrong.

Those few moments that passed before Dr Ajit came to us absolutely killed me. Parveen shot me a confused glance and asked me why the other doctor rushed out like that. I think, at the back of my mind, I knew the answer. I didn't want to say it. I didn't want to believe it. I hoped with all my heart that I was wrong.

Ayaan was oblivious to everything. He had started running around the room and playing with the curtains. Parveen and I sat down. Finally, Dr Ajit walked in and took a chair opposite us, across the table. Ayaan ran up to him and climbed onto his lap. The doctor tried hard to smile, as he held Ayaan delicately. There was a pregnant pause.

My voice quivered. 'D-Doctor? Is everything okay?'

'Your son has a Wilms' tumour,' he said finally. His tone was flat.

'T—tumour?' Parveen stuttered. 'Does that mean it's a . . . *cancer*?'

'Yes, I'm afraid. It's malignant. A rare cancer of the kidneys that primarily affects children.'

Ayaan was at his cheerful best. He was screaming, laughing and playing with Dr Ajit's stethoscope, and running around the room while the latest piece of information hit us like a train. His carefree mood was in stark contrast to the fear that had struck us.

After a few seconds of silence, I could barely manage to let out these words, 'But how, doctor? I don't understand!'

'Wilms' tumours often become quite large before they are noticed,' he continued. 'The newly found Wilms' tumour, on an average, is many times larger than the kidney in which it originates.'

He gave us time to assimilate the information. We couldn't fathom what was happening. I remember looking down at Parveen's hands. She had dug her nails into her skin so hard that she was bleeding a bit. She had lost her bearing completely, and was in an utter daze. My eyes welled up too. *Cancer . . . Tumour . . . These were words I had never thought I would have to hear in my life.*

'We will have to extract the tumour and have him undergo chemotherapy for four months. That's the protocol. I will book a room at the Hinduja Hospital in Mahim. Rush him there right now. Don't delay, we will go into surgery tomorrow itself.'

I excused myself for a bit and stepped out of the room. I passed all the nurses and doctors in the corridor, trying not to let my face betray my emotions. I opened a door and went towards the fire exit. When I knew that I was alone, I finally burst into tears. *It's nothing. We'll get through this. It's nothing.*

I decided to tell Bhatt Sahaab right away. With my hands trembling, I fumbled a bit with the phone before I managed to call him. He answered almost immediately.

'Hey Emmi, has your vacation ended yet or not?' he joked. 'Don't forget you have to get back and shoot!'

I tried to reply sounding as composed as I could. But to no avail. He could hear me sob on the other end.

'Emmi? What happened! Are you crying?' he asked, startled.

'Ayaan has cancer,' I mumbled. 'He has to undergo surgery tomorrow.'

I could tell that Bhatt Sahaab was completely horrified in the silence that ensued.

'Where are you, Emmi? I'll come there! Where are you?'

'Heading home now,' I replied. 'We will take him to Hinduja Hospital in Mahim soon. We need to admit him. Will just go home, pack some stuff and—'

'I'll see you in ten minutes,' he said and disconnected the phone hurriedly.

I went back inside and saw that Parveen and Ayaan were already out of the room with the doctor. By now Parveen was sobbing and Dr Ajit was consoling her by saying it would all be fine, and that we just needed to follow the medical protocol.

'I'll see you at the hospital,' he said. I nodded.

Ayaan looked up at me, his eyes wide and confused. He saw my moist eyes and knew something was wrong. I held him hard against my chest. *My worst fears had been confirmed. And just like that . . . my world came crashing down around me.*

~

I had never driven so fast or so rashly as I did that day. I could see that Parveen was unsuccessfully fighting the urge to cry. Tears flowed down her cheeks as she kept muttering. 'Why him, Emmi? Why him? He's just a little child. What has he done wrong? Did we do something wrong?' We reached our home in five minutes. We tried not to engage in conversation about the illness in front of him.

When we reached home and started packing Ayaan's clothes for the hospital I got an idea. All kids love fairy tales and stories. We decided we would have to lie, script a story for Ayaan's sake. On our return from Bali, Ayaan had kept saying that he wanted to go back. If we told him he was going back to the hospital he would throw a fit. He had already been through the ordeal of a blood test a day before.

'Okay Ayaan,' Parveen said softly, doing her best to put on a smile. 'We're going for another vacation . . . Another holiday . . .'

'Where?' he asked sceptically.

'Bali,' I added. 'You liked the place a lot, didn't you? We're leaving for Bali again.'

My heart sank. He jumped excitedly, running around in the house. We had made the short stop at our place to pack his clothes, before we headed to Mahim to admit him. My family had got the news after my quick call to Bhatt Sahaab. Everyone had come home, dropping everything that they were doing, to be there for us. My parents, Parveen's mom, Bhatt Sahaab, Vikram, Smiley and a few others were waiting in the hall, while Parveen and Ayaan packed his bag in the room. Bhatt Sahaab asked me if the tumour was malignant. His first wife Kiran had had a similar large tumour that turned had out to be benign. I called up Dr Ajit and put him on loudspeaker to confirm the details of the tumour. Bhatt Sahaab was a strong support through those difficult times. I remember him telling Parveen, 'You two have to be strong. Don't ever let him see you cry. Put up a brave front as if everything is okay. *Tum logon ko bachche ke samne acting karni padegi.*'

I stood by myself on the veranda, staring at the serene sea. The rest of the world seemed happy to go about their routine. I suddenly began to dislike everyone and everything. *Why Ayaan? It should've happened to me instead* . . . I called my dad who had left for a health farm in Bengaluru the same morning to take a flight back to Mumbai. I didn't want to tell him about Ayaan, but I'm sure he sensed it.

The rest of my family murmured solemnly amongst themselves. They were all broken. Ayaan is a live wire whom everyone loves. To see him suffer hurt everyone deeply. A tear streamed down my face. And then another. And then, I just broke down completely. This was not a problem I was prepared to handle. I sobbed uncontrollably, letting all the tears flow.

I felt someone's hand on my shoulder. I turned to see Bhatt Sahaab.

'You know, Emmi, I have a great sixth sense.'

I looked back at him, wondering where he was going with this. He paused for a few more moments.

'Nothing's going to happen to your boy,' he said. 'It'll probably be a long battle. But he's going to win it. Everything's going to be fine.'

I nodded, trying to suppress my tears. I wiped my face on my sleeve and walked back into the hall. Parveen and Ayaan were ready. He held his Angry Birds strolley and grinned away. Ayaan always insisted on pulling his own cute small strolley in airports. Today too, with the promise of the excitement of Bali, he packed it himself with all his favourite dinky cars, stuffed toys, especially his favourite stuffed raccoon that he loved hugging and sleeping with. For Ayaan it was his dream come true that he was going back to his favourite holiday destination. We were actually feeling a bit ashamed that we had lied to him, but it was necessary. Bhatt Sahaab held his hand and took him out of the house, near the elevator. I turned to the rest of my family, as they all reassured me that everything was going to be okay. All of them embraced me, one by one. It felt great to have them around. They understood my plight and gave me my space, but also assured me that they were there when I'd need them. Suddenly, we heard a shriek.

We were stunned. It was Ayaan's voice, from near the elevator. And right after that, there was another loud shout. This time it was Bhatt Sahaab! All of us were confused, trying to figure out what was happening. Then there was a third shout, from Ayaan. And following that, another one from Bhatt Sahaab. Each one got louder than the previous. The entire family rushed outside. When we reached the elevator area we saw the two of them indulging in a deafening, boisterous, screaming match which went on for a bit! Our confused faces broke into faint smiles.

Finally, the lift arrived. All of us stepped in, ready to embark on a new journey. Our vehicles waited to take us to the hospital. Bhatt Sahaab looked at me and whispered, 'You heard him scream, didn't you? Emmi, this is life asserting itself. This boy may be three, but he is tough as nails,'

I looked at Ayaan who looked up at me and then at Smiley. He stretched out his arm and gestured for her to pass the water bottle. All that screaming had made him thirsty. After gulping down some water, he stared at the bottle. It had Donald Duck and Daisy Duck gazing at each other fondly. A sly smile crept onto his face. All of us in the lift looked at him.

'If Daddy was on the bottle instead of Donald Duck, he would be kissing Daisy Duck.'

FOUR

MY GIFT AND MY CURSE

15 August 2003. We had decided to release *Footpath* on Independence Day, owing to the fact that it was a holiday and a great opportunity to draw in the audience. It is a difficult emotion to express, how it is to see your film out there in the open, subject to scrutiny. To add to it, it was my debut film. A sense of accomplishment accompanied the butterflies in my stomach. I didn't know what my work would add up to. I was a newcomer with nothing to lose. I knew that if the film didn't click, then I would probably have to try my hand at something else. But I really hoped that the audience liked and accepted me. It was my litmus test. I was a bundle of nerves, albeit a grinning one on the outside. I remember picking up the newspaper in the morning, turning to the film section only to find a picture of myself staring back at me. I checked the show timings for the film at Metro Cinemas—the posh, upscale movie theatre in Marine Lines, South Mumbai.

Along with a couple of close friends, I drove down to the iconic Metro Cinemas. I had bought us tickets in the stall section and waited with the crowd for a bit. The turnout was good. I noticed them looking at the poster and examining the supporting hero they were going to watch for the next two and a half hours. Some of them had good things to say while others not so much.

My friends looked at me, searching for a reaction. I shrugged nonchalantly, returning their scrutinizing gaze with a smile. A few fleeting glances were thrown at me from the crowd too, before the doors opened. Deep down, I was hoping someone would recognize me as we walked in. But thanks to the overdone tan make-up in the poster, nobody did.

We were directed to our seats by the usher. The theatre was packed. The lights went out to the murmur of the audience. I took my seat with bated breath. The titles of the film began to play. My friends and a few others whistled. I got goosebumps.

Seated somewhere in the fourth row, I strained my neck to watch the film intently, as if I didn't know which scene was to follow, which dialogue was next. The audience seemed to be enjoying the movie. The dialogue that I had struggled with, my first dialogue ever, was welcomed with a few shrill whistles. Who would've guessed that that one line had taken me forty-five takes?

Soon, after an engaging first half, it was time for the interval. A popcorn break. I walked out of the theatre and stood casually, with my hands in my pocket. As my friends spoke to each other, I pretended to be part of the conversation. But my mind was elsewhere. I was waiting to be recognized. And then someone spotted me and made the connection.

'Look, he's the guy in the movie! The new one!'

I shrugged, smiling coyly and trying to play it cool.

'Hey, it's Emraan Hashmi!'

'Are you sure?'

Yes, I did look a lot different off screen. The bronzer had given me a darker skin tone in the film. Only on staring for more than a few seconds did people realize that I was the same person they were witnessing on screen.

'The dude playing "Raghu"!'

'Yes, Emraan Hashmi. That's his name!'

I pretended not to hear them, but couldn't help break into a smile. Soon enough, I was giving autographs on tissue papers. The crowd had diverted their attention towards me and I was loving it. As the interval got over, the crowd did not turn and head back inside. Instead, there was a horde of people jostling with each other, stretching their arms out and grabbing me.

I basked in the glory. It was intoxicating. My friends pulled me out of the premises, towards the car park. The crowd followed me out, pouring into the streets. I remember us rushing towards the car and hopping in swiftly. It was only when my friend began to drive did the crowd move away from the car. A few enthusiastic ones ran behind the vehicle as we sped away. I waved at all of them dreamily. That was my first experience of being mobbed and I still remember it vividly. It is a typical movie star experience in India. And I wasn't complaining.

That day left a deep impression on me and the kind of actor I envisioned myself to be. The echoes of the screaming audiences still resonate within me. That was the moment I decided that I wanted to make films for this segment of the audience—the masses. *The single-screen goers.*

In a few minutes, we pulled up at the side of the street, near the Marine Drive promenade by the sea. My friends surprised me with a cake. They cheered as I cut the cake, making passers-by throw us questioning looks.

I still remember the taste of the cake that was meant to celebrate my first brush with fame. It was the taste of stardom. 15 August 2003. It was my Independence Day.

~

The film opened to a lukewarm response and it failed to make any lasting impact on the box office. It didn't make money, but the stage was set—my performance was appreciated by critics and the public alike. A very loyal fan base, especially amongst single-screen goers, germinated post the movie. Suddenly, for them, Emraan Hashmi was someone to take note of. That gave me a high. Everyone at Vishesh Films felt the tremors of my arrival in Bollywood. My family loved *Footpath* too, of course. My grandmother was the proudest, I could tell. 'I told you so,' she would say. Soon enough, I was handed the script of a film titled *Murder* by Bhatt Sahaab.

It was an erotic thriller, something nobody in Bollywood had dared to make before. At Vishesh Films, the Bhatts had the vision to make high-concept, offbeat films with lesser stars, so to speak. They relied on the story and direction rather than letting sheer star power decide the fate of the film. I was the obvious choice for the role of the villainous Sunny. I read the script and loved the menacing grey shades of the character. I was twenty-two at that time, which brought along a separate set of challenges from those demanded of an actor. Challenges like playing this devilish womanizer who was well beyond my years. Moreover, the film had erotic content, in a form that Bollywood hadn't witnessed before. It was intense and bold. Not to forget, highly risqué as well. But the moment I put down that script, I had the gut feeling that I had a potential winner in my hands.

The film was going to be directed by Anurag Basu who had a certain flair for this genre, as displayed earlier on in his career. The film was made on a shoestring budget. A part of it was filmed in Bangkok, but due to budget constraints, the rest was shot back in Mumbai at Anurag's favourite location—the Horizon Hotel in Juhu. Having come from a TV background, where the budgets are even more crunched, Anurag was very good at cheating and making certain places like Horizon Hotel pass off as foreign locales. It was an exhilarating experience, especially the leg in Bangkok, my first ever outdoor schedule.

The story and the performances had to be the real heroes of the film. *Murder* was going to test me in a way that *Footpath* did not. After the platform that was set post *Footpath*, I had to take my talent to the next level. Cast opposite me was Mallika Sherawat, who had three films in her kitty, but nothing that was astoundingly successful. She was touted as a brave and bold actress, which was exactly what this film needed. Though she had done such bold scenes sparingly in the past, even she was new to this level of intense film-making.

As we started out on the film, a few friends indulged in some ribbing, suggesting that I was having a great time filming certain scenes. To be honest though, I was very awkward. Imagine you are out there on a set, pretending to be in love, playacting erotic scenes in front of a posse of crew members, some of who are watching squeamishly, albeit intently. Very few things in life are as uncomfortable. Mallika and I were nervous doing those kissing and simulated sex scenes. Usually Bollywood films tiptoed around the sex scenes, trying to show through implication rather than the act, for instance just showing a couple go into a room, or if they were really risqué, showing them post the act, wrapped up in satin bedsheets. But I didn't watch too many Bollywood films to start with, so again, I had no reference point to follow, especially when it came down to getting sensual on screen. That turned out to be a plus point for me because the biggest reason that *Murder* was a runaway hit was because of its bold content.

I remember shooting my first bold song, '*Bheegey Honth Tere*', in Bangkok. It was set in several locations, but one of them was particularly amusing. Mallika and I were shooting on the top of a parapet of a seven-storey building. After having exhausted every variation and situation that led to the numerous kisses in the song, Anurag wanted us to make out on the ledge of that building! I kept teasing him about how he was making us play out his fantasies on celluloid. So at sundown, when the shooting lights came on, the entire city block came to a halt on the street as they watched us shoot! I'm sure they would have been amused watching two entangled bodies under a sheet snogging away for the camera!

Murder got a bumper opening on 2 April 2004. It was the phase in Bollywood when single-screen goers were predominantly the market who determined the fate of a film. And they simply loved *Murder*. It was the kind of film that they did not know that they wanted to see, until they had seen it. In a country where the portrayal of sex in any form of art is considered a taboo, *Murder* had defied every norm that cinema had established right up to that point. The music of that film was phenomenal and had completely swept the nation. Every rickshaw, every car, every club blasted the catchy '*Kaho Naa Kaho*' and '*Bheegey Honth Tere*'. It was the kind of success that warranted celebration, and this time, I cut a cake at Gaiety-Galaxy Cinemas in Bandra with a huge number of fans, consisting primarily of college kids playing truant, testosterone-charged men and, of course, a lot of women too. If *Footpath* was the film that got me noticed, *Murder* was the film that rocketed me to a level of stardom that I couldn't imagine. I wasn't even aware of the definition of stardom back then. Some people in this ruthless film industry did not want to label or accept me as a bona fide star because I had none of the clichéd trappings of a Bollywood hero. Despite this, the film raked in the numbers, made great profits and established Emraan Hashmi (or in some cases, 'the *Murder* guy') as a household name.

The film had its fair share of detractors too, as any piece of creative work is bound to find. I read every review, because back then, I was new to the world. I would feel a little dejected now and then, if I came across a bad one. Some industry pundit said that the film worked only because of the sexual content even though I know for a fact that the audience enjoyed the plot. Someone even said that I resembled a monkey, but that was something I laughed off. Four years later, incidentally, the same critic turned up at my doorstep to offer me a film. I politely refused. The film bombed without a trace. I'm sure he realized that it's easier to sit in judgement and criticize than to get down to actually making a film.

At a time when Bollywood was all about family films, comedies, action–masala movies, *Murder* broke all stereotypes. It was touted by some as 'soft pornography', which is not exactly true. It brought a very negative connotation to the film. I agree that it had erotic content, but so do a million films in Hollywood. In fact, there are scenes which are genuinely pornographic out there, but these same people would heap praises upon such foreign films and appreciate the story. The hypocrisy was laughable. I am not saying that *Murder* is a masterpiece, but I didn't comprehend the 'holier than thou' attitude of some detractors who said that kissing was vulgar and in bad taste. These are the same people who would harp another tune if they saw Sharon Stone's *Basic Instinct.* I would not give in to such frustrations, but it did afford me a reality check about the sensitivities and hypocrisies of some people in the name of culture. To be honest, I had no qualms about doing this sort of a film because I did not feel I was violating any moral code of conduct. Besides, in the process, we had tapped into an entire new market out there who loved the movie. The film was a game changer for Vishesh Films, even though I had been accused of single-handedly contaminating Indian cinema!

After *Murder,* I was offered several films by other banners too. It was a great position to be in. I had finally tasted success. It was, as Bhatt Sahaab put it, *the birth of a star . . .*

~

It was eight in the morning. I watched my friend from the shadows of the corridor. He stepped out of his hotel room, ready to go to the gym. *Now is the time . . .* Once he was away, I walked up to the door casually and swiped it open with the keycard I had obtained a few minutes ago from the front desk. I had managed to convince the local Mauritian manager that I was sharing the room with my friend, despite having one booked under my name. He didn't argue much once one of the Indian boys pulled him aside and told him that I was the lead actor of the film that was being shot in the premises.

'I'll give it back to you in five minutes,' I promised earnestly. 'I've just forgotten my glasses inside.'

Well, here I was. Inside my friend's room. I walked in stealthily and switched on the lamp. I opened the cupboard where I thought he kept his clothes and made a mental note of the order of the things. I tried to find what I had come for without being messy. Couldn't find it. For someone who had joined us a couple of days back, he had already shopped a lot. I decided to throw caution to the winds and just rummaged through the neat pile until I found what I was looking for at the bottom. I tugged it out, slammed the cupboard door hastily after arranging the clothes the way I had found them, and walked out of the room.

I returned the keycard at the front desk, walked up to my own room and closed the door behind me. I breathed a sigh of relief after my morning adventure. I looked at the time. It was eight-thirty. In about half an hour we were going to start filming the footage for the trailer of my film, an adult comedy—*Jawani Deewani*. As per the shot, I was supposed to swagger in with my back towards the camera and then turn around and smile. Let's just say I had found a way to make that shot a whole lot more interesting . . .

When I walked onto the set soon after, which was on a beautiful beach of Mauritius, the director Manish Sharma was really happy to see what I had brought along.

'Well, I worked hard for it!' I joked. 'Let's do the shot before my friend notices his favourite T-shirt has gone missing! I just stole it from his room!'

After a single take, we got it right. I went up to the screen and saw the shot. I walked into the frame and immediately the two words came into focus. *Serial Kisser.*

Just the previous night, when my friend showed me the green full-sleeved T-shirt that he had picked up at the local market, I had hardly paid any attention to it. It was only when he held the T-shirt right in front of my face did I realize what it said. We laughed for a bit, until everyone in the lobby turned to look at us.

'Dude, if anyone should be wearing this in our country, it's me.'

By then, I had done at least five movies which were punctuated with bold, erotic scenes.

'Well, I'm not giving it to you if that's what you're hinting at,' he said quickly.

'What if I wear it just the one time?' I asked. 'For my film?'

But he wouldn't hear of it. He was halfway to his room already. Well, let's just say he wasn't too pleased when he saw the rushes of the trailer.

'Thanks Emmi,' he said, sourly. 'Now everyone will think I'm copying you if I ever wear this. Thank you, serial kisser!'

I had laughed at it then, but hadn't realized that I had dug myself a deep grave. Little did I know that a decade down the line I would still be tagged as the 'Serial Kisser' by the media. It was a convenient name and had they come up with it themselves, I think I would have taken it in my stride. But here, in a bout of mischief, I had fed them this moniker myself. It was my mess and I was entirely to blame. Don't get me wrong, I did not really have much of a problem with the tagline. In fact, it helped me with certain films. A large chunk of the audience wants to see Emraan Hashmi, the Serial Kisser. But at the same time I feel it trivializes what I do on screen which is more than just a few kissing scenes. Usually the roles I do have stories to tell. But in the end, it's those kissing scenes that grab the headlines. And in the few films that

I didn't kiss, that was the point highlighted by the media. It is a catch-22 situation, so to speak.

I had created this image that I found tough to break out of. In fact, some directors always slip in a kissing scene after my first reading of the script. In most cases, these kisses defied logic, just like the insertion of a song into a narrative. But then we give the audiences what they crave for, even if it is outside the realm of logic. And apparently, they'd rather take an 'Emraan Hashmi Chartbuster' and a few Emraan Hashmi kisses over a sensible plotline. I have seen some of my films in theatres around the country. There is usually a build-up of three minutes—a prelude to the kiss—which is when you'll hear the loudest hooting and clapping that often drowns out the dialogues. I guess that's the price my directors have to pay.

I have also witnessed that among the films where I haven't kissed, a few have done well, and more than a few have left the theatres without a trace. But these kiss-less films annoy a section of the audiences to an immeasurable extent. They feel cheated and make their displeasure very apparent by booing and screaming out: '*Kiss kyon nahin kar raha hai be? Bimaar hai kya?*' (Why aren't you kissing? Are you ill?). I have since learned that when I'm in a film, it's a part of the formula to include a kissing scene. Very few producers and directors are willing to take the chance of not having me cosy up to the heroine. Just as Shah Rukh Khan strikes his trademark pose with his arms outstretched or Salman loses his shirt to reveal his abs, Emraan Hashmi kisses his heroines passionately, much to the delight of the jubilant audiences.

Kissing is also a lot more common now than it was when I had entered the scene. I didn't think it had shock value when I started off but obviously I was mistaken. I didn't think about it too much but people around were more conservative than I was. However, there's no shock value attached to it any more. Every actor, old or new, has done it at some point. Almost all films nowadays have intimate scenes. The novelty has worn off. But film-makers always play it safe when it comes to me. Regardless of the others, I will always wear the crown of the Serial Kisser. I don't mind it, but I don't mind not having it on my head either.

Some people have the general misconception that I enjoy shooting erotic scenes. It's really not that easy. I'm always conscious before I pucker up. It's one thing to do it in the confines of your room with your own partner, but quite another to be playing it out on a set in front of a whole crew scrutinizing your every move and a director who gives you instructions on how to go about it. If anyone thinks it's a dream job, they're sadly mistaken. The sexy kiss on screen seems like the unsexiest thing off screen. Most of the time there is awkward teeth clanking with the director yelling, 'Show your face, Emi. Your face is getting covered by your hair.' And the most irritating one, 'Guys, your make-up is all over the sheets. We will have to change them. Let's break for lunch.' I mean, sure, I get to kiss these beautiful women and all of that . . . but it does get boring. Either ways, it's a burden I bear and will continue to do so . . . willingly. And like it or not, after more than a hundred and fifty kisses (I've lost count), it's not easy to dethrone me as the Kissing King or Chumban Devta as a crowd that had gathered for one of my film shoots in Delhi started shouting. Spider Man says it best: *It is my gift and it is my curse.*

My mum, Maherah, and dad, Anwar

In my father's arms

With my mother, back in the day!

Me as a toddler,
enjoying my birthday!

The carefree days flew by!

My grandmother, Purnima

Ayaan with his friend   The play park was his escape

Off-road ride with Ayaan

Mommy and Ayaan   A family selfie!
love their selfies!

My first shot in *Footpath*

Once Upon a Time in Mumbai . . .

My look in *Gangster:*
A Love Story

Parveen and I when we had just
begun dating

The Bali New Year trip, before Ayaan fell ill

Family selfie in Bali

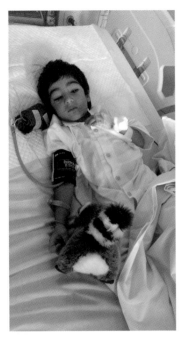

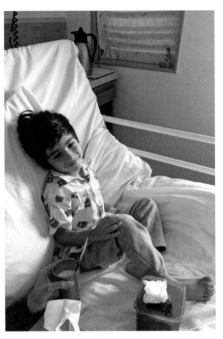

The making of a superhero

Cheerful even on the hospital bed!

Even thinking about the tumour sends a shudder down my spine.
This monster grew inside my little son.

The superhero party!

I'm Batman!

Superhero kids!

Ayaan's first superhero birthday party after we
came back, 3 February 2015

'At least now I can have some cake, Dad! It's sugar free!'

Chuck E. Cheese with his little fan!

Selfie with Mommy

Theatre time

Nothing can bog Ayaan down

FIVE

THE FIRST STEP TO BECOMING IRON MAN

'It's 4.30 a.m.! Do you have any bloody sense?' My lips quivered as I spewed out these words venomously. 'Any etiquette at all? This is a damn hospital! There are little children sleeping here . . . There are patients who need to rest! You bunch of idiots!'

Parveen interrupted my outburst by tugging at my arm and pulling me out of the hospital kitchen.

Just a few moments earlier, I was sitting beside Ayaan's hospital bed, watching him sleep. He had his first chemotherapy session scheduled in a couple of days. I was lost in thoughts, wondering about the sudden twist of events and what fate had in store for me next when suddenly I heard a loud Hindi expletive from the adjacent kitchen. Following it was another chain of abuses someone else hurled back at the first guy. I looked at Parveen, who just shrugged and gestured to me to let it be. And then we heard loud peals of laughter. I stood up abruptly, ready to go out and have a word with those responsible for the ruckus.

'Let it be, Emmi. There's nothing you can do about it,' Parveen said resignedly.

As soon as she said this, there was the loud clang caused by a steel utensil hitting the ground. That was the last straw.

'Well, let's see!'

I pushed past her and walked into the kitchen, my eyes bloodshot with sleep deprivation and now, anger. I gave them a piece of my mind. The staff in the kitchen hung their heads in shame, a great fabricated show of regret as I growled at them. I was seething with rage and had Parveen not intervened, I would have picked up the steel vessel that lay on the ground and clobbered their heads with it. Mind you, I'm not a violent person at all. But when someone messes with the well-being of my kid, especially in the state that he was in then, I am bound to see red.

We were in the paediatric ward of the hospital, where a lot of kids were resting after being operated upon or after their chemotherapy sessions, or were soon to go in for surgeries or treatments. And this little rest was very crucial for them, mentally and physically.

It had been almost a week since the tumour had been extracted along with the kidney by the skilful surgeon—Dr Ravi Ramadwar. Ayaan's recovery post the operation was surprisingly fast. We were all preparing ourselves to watch him being confined to bed for at least a week. Instead, he was back on his feet in three days. The urge to jump out of bed and play with his remote-control cars overpowered any physical discomfort. He was running around in the corridors of Hinduja, with us tailing him and asking him to slow down.

Parveen and I were understandably anxious when the reports came in. We were hoping his tumour would be in the first stage. Unfortunately, we were told it was in the second. This upstaging was quite a nightmare. But in this particular case, there wouldn't have been much of a difference in the methods of treatment. We also prayed that the tumour was a favourable one as an unfavourable tumour could cause severe complications. Luckily enough, it was favourable. We were told the cancer had also affected his renal calyces, which are the outlet chambers of the kidneys through which urine passes to the bladder. The oncologist had stated that at the centre of a tumour, the level of oxygen is low. So when a tumour is cut, for its own survival, it starts pouring out cells to multiply and survive. These cells then lodge themselves onto other organs and pose the danger of making those organs cancerous as well. Therefore, the tumour is usually cut off. In Ayaan's case, however, the tumour had enveloped the kidney completely, so it had to be removed along with the kidney. The doctors had unsuccessfully tried to save his kidney. To further ensure that the cancer wouldn't spread, we were informed, Ayaan would have to undergo multiple cycles of chemotherapy. And the toughest truth about chemotherapy is that, in a bid to kill the cancer, often there is collateral damage. Besides numerous other side effects, it inevitably weakens the immune system. Also, there is the possibility of the cancer recurring. For us parents, who couldn't bear to see as much as a cut on our child, it was a daunting road ahead.

The week that followed was full of sleepless nights and unbearable paranoia. When I had first heard the diagnosis, I had broken down, which is natural for anyone hearing about a loved one suffering from a terminal illness. But after a point, I switched into battle mode. I gathered as much information as I could, made a million phone calls and resolved to do everything that it would take to save Ayaan's life. I recall vividly the night after Ayaan's surgery. He was still groggy with the morphine, and Parveen and I would take turns to sleep with him in the recovery ward. I got many calls from everyone I had worked with professionally and a few others. John Abraham was one of the first few to call. He told me about his dad who had been diagnosed, but was cancer-free now. Sanjay Dutt and his family also called me up and reassured me that nothing would happen to my boy. Sanjay and Priya Dutt spoke of the Memorial Sloan Kettering Cancer Center in New York. I also found support in Indian cricketer Yuvraj Singh who had heroically braved cancer and had bounced back to an

everyday life. It was extremely sweet of him to pass on advice
and even connect us to the facility at which he was treated. He
even brought back some vitamins from abroad that were essential
for Ayaan's recovery. Another person I found of great help was
Akshay Kumar.

I first met Akshay at an Eid party that was also a build-up to
the film *Once Upon a Time in Mumbai 2*. This was a film that
I was associated with in the past, and my character of a feared
underworld figure—Shoaib—was now being reprised by Akshay.
As soon as I stepped in, Akshay greeted me with a bone-crunching
hug and a firm handshake.

'I'm glad we've finally met,' he said with a friendly grin.
'Whoever has spoken about you, always tells me that we are both
quite alike. We are punctual, we share a similar work ethic, we
have similar ways of handling our money, and many other such
commonalities.'

'And we've both played the role of Shoaib,' I joked.

That evening, in 2013, was great. I had certainly made a
friend. Akshay and I were indeed similar in many ways. But the
one thing that we didn't share then, but do share now, was the
anguish of having a close family member battle cancer.

Exactly a year and a half later, when Ayaan was recovering
from his first surgery (the tumour removal), my phone buzzed
briefly. I saw a text that read, 'Hi, this is Akshay Kumar. Please
call when you're free.' I called back immediately.

'Hi Emraan,' he said softly. 'Is it true? What I read about your
son?'

'Yes,' I whispered. 'We've gotten the tumour removed
successfully. Couldn't save the kidney, so that was extracted as well.'

'How long are you going to be there at the hospital?' he asked.
'I'll come there.'

I was touched.

'No sir,' I said. 'It's okay. Things are under control. Besides, you must be tied up with work.'

'If you need anything, I'm a phone call away, okay? I know some good doctors and facilities. *Kuch bhi chahiye bata de!*'

After that phone call, he called me every day to follow up on Ayaan. After Ayaan was brought back home, he called up once and asked, 'Where's your son?'

'He's home now,' I replied.

'I'm coming,' he said.

Akshay reached my place within the hour. Ayaan was advised as much rest as possible, and so he was asleep that afternoon. Once he arrived, we tiptoed into Ayaan's room. Akshay walked towards him and looked at Ayaan's angelic face. He was fast asleep. Akshay's eyes then shifted to the large poster on the wall of Ayaan in his Bat-Suit. I noticed his eyes brimming with tears. He gently caressed Ayaan's head and then turned to me.

'How old is he?'

'He's going to be four soon,' I replied. He turned back and looked at Ayaan fondly.

We walked out of the room and had a brief conversation in the living room. This is when I realized that he had lost his father to cancer a few years ago. I understood right away why he empathized with me. This is what cancer does to you. Once it invades your home, it changes you completely. There's a sudden paradigm shift in the way you look at things. The news of someone else's diagnosis sends a shiver down your spine and you are instantly connected to the pain. You want to do everything you can to help.

Akshay mentioned Canada as a place that I should consider for Ayaan's treatment. He told me that he could easily organize lodging and other amenities for me out there. When he left my house, I remember making a mental note to tell Ayaan that Akshay Kumar had come to visit him.

During the phase that followed the tumour extraction, I spent time researching some other paediatric hospitals and institutes where I could take Ayaan for his chemotherapy after the first session at Hinduja Hospital. I had zeroed in on two such hospitals—St. Jude Children's Research Hospital in Memphis recommended by my friend Sharan's father and SickKids in Canada. I wanted to get the primary cycle of chemo out of the way after which I would whisk him off to one of these institutes. It is not good to skip or delay treatment for any illness. The entire procedure that Ayaan would have to undergo, the doctor informed me in one of our numerous sittings, was going to be a six-month-long affair.

Ayaan would be under constant medical surveillance. When he was awake, he showed no signs of being ill. He would chatter non-stop and be his spunky self. Occasionally, the weakness would overcome him and he would break down. He would question why he was in the hospital and why we weren't in Bali as we had promised him. And I would rush off to another room, call Parveen's phone which displayed the Batman symbol when I called from a particular number. She would then show it to him to stop him from crying and let him answer the phone.

'H—Hello,' his voice would tremble. 'Is that Batman?'

And I would try hard to stick to the script, and do my best voice impersonation of the Dark Knight with a lump in my throat.

'Yes,' I would say. 'You are a brave boy, Ayaan. Very soon, you'll be a superhero too!'

And soon enough, the crying would subside and he would be playing with his toys again. In those few days, the Internet had consumed me entirely. As I had stated earlier, it's the best and the worst place to be at. I read almost everything—articles and literature—that there was on the Wilms' tumour, on cancer in general and of course on the other dreaded 'C-word' that comes along with the deadly illness—chemotherapy.

~

From what I was told by the doctors and what I had gathered from the books that I had read along with the articles available on the Internet, my understanding of chemotherapy had broadened considerably. For those who aren't in the know, chemotherapy is a type of treatment that uses inorganic drugs to destroy cancer cells. It stops or slows the growth of such cells, which would otherwise fester, grow and divide quickly. The downside, however, involves collateral damage to some healthy cells as well. These are usually the cells that divide quickly, the ones that form the lining of the mouth, the intestines and even the cells that cause hair to grow. Some chemo drugs cause adverse reactions that affect the heart at a later stage in a person's life. If Ayaan had been diagnosed at stage 3, he would have had to take one of those lethal drugs. The promising part in Ayaan's case, however, is that the side effects get better or go away completely post the treatment.

Chemotherapy is subjective, it varies from case to case. There are different kinds of medicines that are available, different methods of administration, and so on and so forth. The treatment is known to cure cancer, that is, it destroys the multiplying cancer cells to the point that they can no longer be detected and are unlikely to grow back. And it has a high success rate too, depending upon the age of the person and the stage of the cancer, especially in children with relapsed/recurrent diseases. The younger the patient, the lower the stage, the higher is the probability of success. Chemo also shrinks tumours that cause pain or pressure. This is known as palliative care.

Had Ayaan not undergone the chemo treatment after the surgery, the chances of metastatic cancer, which spreads to other parts of the body, would have been highly possible. The chemo was supposed to keep the cancer from spreading, despite the tumour having been extracted. The medication was supposed to slow the growth until it destroyed the cancer cells completely, thus preventing it from spreading to other parts of the body.

The doctors usually decide the chemo drugs depending on what kind of cancer the patient has. There is no fixed method of going about treating this tricky ailment, which is why it is so dreadful. It has the ability of completely blowing up in your face, if not treated correctly at the first go itself. The chemo drugs that the doctor had prescribed for Ayaan's treatment were vincristine and dactinomycin. They were to be administered intravenously (IV), that is, directly into his veins. These drugs had some shocking side effects that included hair loss, constipation, peripheral neurotherapy—that is an often irreversible condition featuring pain, numbness, sensitivity, mouth ulcers—and conditions where the limbs almost become limp with intense pins and needles. Besides, if even a drop of the medication is spilt onto the patient's skin, it would burn and blacken that patch. The liquid was that potent . . . *that poisonous.* Chemo medicines have often been equated with poison. Scanning through more notes and documents made me believe that to be true. It is a necessary evil. I remember slamming the laptop shut in fear at this point. Reading about chemotherapy only worsened my fears.

Even though the literature around cancer was scaring the living daylights out of me, I was hungry for more information. I would sit in Ayaan's hospital room, plug in my earphones and watch documentaries about the disease on my iPad. I wanted to know everything that existed about this illness, and had even started reading Indian-born American oncologist Siddhartha Mukherjee's detailed book, *The Emperor of All Maladies*, that even won a Pulitzer for general non-fiction. The only time I put all of this away was when I waited nervously while Ayaan underwent his first chemo session. In fact, I was so consumed by all the reading material and documentaries that I had gathered a great deal of information and had all my questions prepared for the various doctors that I had consulted. Some of them were taken aback by the questions I shot at them and told me that they would get back with the answers. *Too much information will stress you out,* they said. *Leave it to us.* But I couldn't. I wanted to know he was going to be okay. I wanted to know everything and do everything to help. Otherwise I wouldn't have been able to forgive myself.

~

Ayaan's first chemotherapy session took place at noon a week after his surgery. He was administered the dactinomycin by Dr Sagar, a very friendly and jovial man at Hinduja Hospital. Ayaan was very fond of his nurse, Aparna, and she could make Ayaan do the things he was otherwise unwilling to do. Aparna slowly injected the syringe into his arm through which the drug would be administered intravenously. Dr Sagar took over from there. The procedure didn't last for more than ten minutes. Parveen and I diverted his attention with the iPad. That night, once we took him home, we were on our toes. I had already read up a lot and knew of the side effects that were going to pop up. All was fine till around eight at night when he had a light dinner. Then he started feeling uneasy, complained of nausea and cried as he vomited a bit. Apart from that, not much happened. But this was just the start. The tiny puncture on his arm made my heart bleed. I recalled that moment again, when I was thinking of ways to sidestep a routine vaccination. I had realized that uncertainty is the most common element of life. I did not want him to go through any pain. I wanted to ease the agony, but I was helpless.

~

Earlier in the day, a few hours after the first dose of chemo was administered, I remember sitting with Parveen outside Ayaan's ward. Both of us were quiet and did not want to speak, and if at all we did had to speak, we only turned to one another, nobody else. I looked her in the eye and told her of my plans.

'I've found out about two good hospitals in the US and Canada,' I said. 'We should get him out of here. The doctors are great, but the environment doesn't help.'

She seemed to agree. I went on to elaborate.

'The pollution, the weather, none of it is in his favour,' I said. 'I'm not willing to take that risk. I have spoken to a few doctors about this too and they have recommended the same names to me—St. Jude and SickKids.'

She knew I was leaning towards Canada, because Parveen had family there. It would mean that we wouldn't be in a foreign country entirely alone. I could see that she was toying with the idea, ready to give in. It would be an additional stress, no doubt. Packing everything up and leaving for another country. But she was completely in sync with where I was coming from. Later that night, she came into Ayaan's room again. She gestured that we have the conversation outside, or else we would wake him up. He was fatigued and nauseous, and drifting in and out of sleep would have been detrimental.

'What about work?' she asked me, as we sat on the chairs outside his room. 'The schedules?'

'I've spoken to Vikram,' I replied, telling her about the status of his film *Mr X*. 'He had pulled down one set without consulting me. They've incurred some losses according to my calculations but nothing that insurance can't cover.'

She closed her eyes and breathed in. I continued.

'The other producers, UTV, are currently rethinking the fate of *Raja Natwarlal*. They don't think it will happen this year. Even

Hamari Adhuri Kahani . . . But since that is under the Vishesh Films banner it might still be possible to play around with those dates.'

My voice was shaky. She knew I was in a major dilemma. I could not walk out of the films. Despite everyone having pledged their support and offered help, I knew it would not have been a sound professional move to pull out. My value would have dropped in the film circles. We work in a cut-throat industry. Besides, everyone had kitchens to run, right from the spot boys to the make-up men to my co-actors. Pulling out or even postponing the schedules would have hurt them all. And everything considered, if I were to take Ayaan abroad for his treatment, that would've cost us a lot of money too.

'What will you do about that, Emraan? You cannot cancel the shoots. There's a lot of money at stake!'

I gave her an affirmative nod and let out a deep breath. In hindsight, I look at it as the greatest test of my character. I was torn between two important aspects of my life, and I could neglect neither. I needed to strike a balance.

'I won't,' I said finally. 'I'll complete my schedules, as promised.'

She smiled tiredly.

'And do you really want to take him to Canada?'

And then, as if on cue, we heard the unmistakable sound of a steel vessel hit the floor and bounce around, followed by the cussing of the raucous kitchen staff. 'Do you still want me to answer that?'

~

When I met Anurag Basu he told me about his successful battle with leukaemia. He reassured me that Ayaan would be fine in no time, and since the tumour was out there was nothing to worry.

He gave me the number of a certain Dr Shripad Banavali who had helped him win the fight with cancer.

Dr Shripad Banavali worked at the Tata Memorial Hospital. Situated in the heart of Parel, the hospital is a centre for the prevention, treatment, education and research on cancer. It is recognized as one of the leading cancer centres in India. The Tata hospital was large and had a couple of wings. The general environment at the hospital was grim, as I learnt when I visited it much later. Children were resting on the floor, right after their chemo sessions. Their parents, not privileged enough, were waiting by them misty eyed, holding onto nothing but strings of hope. There was a huge crowd of people of all ages, assembled in the middle of one of the sections of the hospital. They were united by two fatal things—cancer and poverty. They were probably being treated via the money that came in through donations. Chemotherapy is an expensive process. It was then that I made up my mind to do as much as I could for those who suffer from this illness. I thanked the one above for the smallest privileges in my life, which I had earlier shunned or not even considered as blessings. As clichéd as it may seem, walking through that hospital made me realize that one shouldn't take little things in life for granted.

I had a word with Dr Banavali on the phone, telling him that I wanted to consult him for Ayaan's treatment. I was told by Anurag that he is one of the best people to talk to, especially since he had saved Anurag's life after he was diagnosed with fourth-stage leukaemia.

He agreed to meet me right away. And instead of me having to go to him, he decided to come and see me at Hinduja itself. We met at the canteen, of all places.

'Good evening,' I greeted Dr Banavali. He walked towards me briskly with an outstretched arm. Dr Banavali struck me as a very pleasant man. He had a calm, matter-of-fact expression that was in stark contrast to all the horrors he might have seen at the

Tata Hospital wards. He met with about a hundred terminally ill people of different age groups from different parts of the country every day. 'I'm Emraan. We spoke on the phone.'

'So I believe you want to take your son to St. Jude's for treatment?'

'That's correct,' I replied. I went on to tell him about Ayaan's ailment, and how we had gotten his tumour removed. I added that I did not want to take any chances with him and the remaining cycles. He agreed. I also mentioned SickKids as an option. I told him Canada was where I wanted Ayaan to be treated because we had family and acquaintances there. He assured me that he would connect me to both these institutes.

Soon, we finalized our decision to get Ayaan admitted to SickKids in Toronto. It was the more practical option of the two, and they had replied to my email reassuringly, saying that they were ready to treat Ayaan.

~

We helped Ayaan out of the car; we had brought him back home. He was frail but thrilled at the idea of getting back. He thought it was all done. Sadly, he was mistaken. But we weren't going to burst his bubble. Not yet. The poor kid needed a break, so Parveen and I had planned a little something for him. As he got into the lift, I lifted him in my arms. Parveen and I shot each other a quick look. She nodded and smiled. I rang the bell.

The door swung open. I put Ayaan down and he stepped in. And then suddenly, there was a loud cheer! All his friends came running towards him. He was overjoyed. He clapped and laughed ecstatically.

'Welcome back, Ayaan!'

As he walked in, he saw some new superhero figurines in addition to the previous ones, all arranged on the table, waiting to be played with. There was a large Batman poster hanging from the ceiling, smack in the middle of the hall. The other wall was covered with another poster, the Bat symbol. And yet another wall was adorned with a poster of Iron Man. The soundtrack of the film *Dark Knight* played in the background. Parveen had organized this little surprise superhero party. She had gotten special cards printed and sent them to his friends, inviting them over to come dressed as superheroes. Vineet, Smiley's husband, had made a photoshopped poster of Ayaan wearing a mask like Batman's at his office that was used as an e-invite for a superhero get-together. It was pretty cool. The poster had a mishmash of grabs from various superhero movies and candid photos of Ayaan that I had shot. The parents of the invitees probably already knew about Ayaan's ailment, as several newspapers had run the story. They were all very supportive, as were the teachers at his school. Everyone had turned up, and were glad to see him.

Ayaan, despite his weakness, was hard to contain. He would run up to his friends and chat animatedly with them. I would keep a constant watch, so as to not let him exert himself too much. The only thing missing from the party was junk food. Chips, pizzas, cake, soda, the whole lot. I had read up a lot about such stuff facilitating cancer, and I was never going to let him touch them again. For now, he was thrilled to see his friends after almost ten days.

'So when are you coming back to school?'

'Soon,' he replied excitedly.

Little did he know he was going to be off again to a faraway country for a long, long time.

That evening, after Ayaan's friends had left, he got another call from Batman. Parveen had placed her mobile strategically in front of him so that when it rang the Batman symbol would flash before his eyes. I called the phone and kept my mobile aside. He looked at the phone, then at Parveen and then at me.

'Is it a call for you, Ayaan?'

He looked at me wide-eyed and nodded. He lifted the phone and walked away to his room, sheepishly. Once he was inside, he answered it.

'Hello Batman!' he exclaimed. 'I am back home!'

'How did you like the party that I kept for you, Ayaan? I had invited all your friends!'

He laughed. It was music to my ears.

'So Ayaan,' I growled away. 'I wanted to tell you that the first step of becoming Iron Man is now complete. Just a few more steps after which you will become a superhero!'

I sounded a bit too excited, but he did not catch my bluff. He fell silent.

'More steps?' he asked, cautiously.

'Yes,' I replied. 'We will go to Canada to make you a superhero. Are you ready, Ayaan?'

There was a pregnant pause. He mulled over this bit of news. I was worried that I had worded the question wrongly. *What if he wasn't ready?* I was going to say it again and this time try to make it sound like an order. But before I could say anything, he replied feebly.

'Yes. I am ready.'

SIX

TRACING THE ROOTS

'What is the actual purpose of your visit, sir?' the official asked the man seated opposite him. His eyes were doubtful, his tone curt.

The man shrugged. He had been waiting at the High Commission of Pakistan—the Pakistani Embassy—for a good two hours before it was his turn to apply for a visa. They had known that the man would be coming in and were informed well in advance by the Indian officials. Despite that, they made him wait, and once his turn came, they fired the same questions at him repeatedly. They could not be blamed though. It was 1986 and relations between the two countries—India and Pakistan— were strained. Every Indian who wanted to fly to Pakistan was scanned thoroughly and vice versa. Neither of the countries could be too sure.

'I've told you already,' the man replied. 'I work in the commercial department of Air India. Prime Minister Rajiv Gandhi will be flying over Karachi and I have to get the overflying rights in place. I am merely following protocol.'

The officials thought the man had a different agenda. But they were compelled to hand him his visa anyway due to political pressure from the Indians. The man's job, once he reached Pakistan, was pretty straightforward and would've taken him a couple of days at most. He was supposed to stay in Karachi until Rajiv Gandhi's flight flew over the city. It was important for him to remain there just in case the flight needed to land due to an emergency. Luckily, everything went off smoothly. The man returned to India from Pakistan. The man in question was Anwar Hashmi, my father.

My father always begins this tale with the scene at the embassy. I was seven when this happened to him. He would tell me about how that short work trip to Karachi got him wondering about where in Pakistan his estranged father, who had left him and his mother in 1951, was. He was seven at that time, and I was intrigued to know more about my paternal grandfather—Shaukat Hashmi.

'That initial work trip to Karachi was a catalyst,' my father would say later on, once I had grown up and was capable of deeper understanding. I would sit by him and listen to him recounting the days he decided to live out an adventure. 'After returning to India from the work trip, I realized that I wanted to go back to Pakistan and find my father. My father who had left me when I was a little kid.'

And that is exactly what he did. In a couple of months, he went back to Karachi. It had been a few years short of three decades since he had seen his father last. He did receive the occasional letter from him though, written in impeccable handwriting and perfect English. His father was a journalist and writer, who had left his wife—Meher—when my dad was seven. But barring the few letters, there was no other contact between them. My father decided to change that.

With a vague mental image of what Shaukat Hashmi looked like that he had gathered from an old picture of his, my father set out on a journey that took him from Karachi to Lahore. My father had learned that my grandfather had remarried a Jewish woman with whom he had a daughter. He asked around, gathering bits of information until he finally stepped into a slightly crowded marketplace. It was evening and he was physically exhausted, enquiring for the address of a certain Shaukat Hashmi. But finally, his perseverance bore fruit as he stood opposite a dilapidated one-storey bungalow. His legs shook slightly as he walked towards the house. A youth, who looked slightly younger than twenty-five, was about to climb onto his cycle. My father walked up to him and tapped him on the shoulder.

'Yes, how may I help you?' the boy asked him hurriedly.

'Is this Shaukat Hashmi's house?'

'Yes, the door is open. Go in and up the staircase,' the boy replied. 'He's on the first floor.'

My father pushed open the door and took a step inside. There were butterflies in his stomach. After travelling all the way, he was having second thoughts. *Should he? Shouldn't he?* He went up the staircase anyway, until he reached a closed door. His finger hovered over the doorbell. After a few long seconds, he pressed it. He always takes a moment to swallow at this point, when he recollects the memories and narrates the incident to anyone.

The door creaked open. The room was dimly lit. A man in a light green pathaani suit roughly my father's height stood right in front of him. Anwar Hashmi and Shaukat Hashmi looked at each other, as time stood still. It was a touching moment, the kind you'd see in a film. But it was as real as it could get.

'*Aa gaye naa tum, aakhir mein.*' Shaukat Hashmi was the first to break the silence. '*Aa hi gaye.* You have come, finally.'

They embraced each other soon after. They looked very similar, their facial features almost indistinguishable. Soon, my grandfather introduced his son to his new family—his wife, two sons (one was the boy with the cycle) and one daughter. They were extremely friendly towards my father, exchanging contact details and clicking photographs. Since my father was slated to leave the next day, the others in the family left the two men to themselves, allowing them to catch up and make up for lost time.

They spoke about numerous things. My grandfather told my father about his career as a journalist, a writer and even about his stint as a film director in Pakistan. He had become a man of influence, but he still had a chequered career. Nothing consistent, nothing concrete. It was just how he was in all aspects of his life, I guess. My dad in turn updated him about his life, probably told him about me too. But my grandfather was more interested to know about his former wife. He stressed upon why he did not like her choice of career, her new producer husband, the glitzy-glamorous world of stardom that is as thin as a veil. But he could not have had much of a say, despite his strong opinion. He was the one who had got up and left her.

Before leaving, the next morning, my father and grandfather walked to the mosque and offered namaz. My father still chuckles at the fact that his half-brothers did not pray along with them. At the end of the namaz, my grandfather asked him to visit them again.

'Anwar, I hope to see you again.'

My father agreed. But the next time he went to Pakistan, a couple of years later, he could not find the family. They had shifted as it was a rented house. Nobody knew where they had gone. No contact, no address. Father was forced to return without meeting them this time. His only solace lay in the fact that he had met his father and his new family at least once after they were separated. In 1992 he was informed that Shaukat Hashmi had passed away.

~

My paternal grandmother, Meher Bano, was, as Bhatt Sahaab puts it, the first star of the family. She started her acting career at the young age of fourteen and worked for over three decades, and was one of the most dynamic actresses of her era, with more than a hundred films to her credit. Her transformation from Meher Bano to Purnima Varma is a story she always told me in bits and pieces.

Born in Mumbai on 2 March 1932, Meher Bano's father Ram Sheshadri Ayengar was a Tamil Brahmin. He worked as an accountant at the office of film distributor Kiku Bhai Desai (iconic film-maker Manmohan Desai's father). Her mother was from a Muslim family in Lucknow. She had four sisters and a brother. Her eldest sister, Shirin, is Bhatt Sahaab's mother and had already acted in a few films.

At that time, our neighbour was a prominent director of that era—Raman B. Desai. When my grandmother was still in school, and was around fourteen years old, she was offered the role of Radha in Raman B. Desai's Gujarati film *Radheshyam*. For the film, Desai gave her the alias of Purnima, to use as her screen name. That was the trend of the era, where actors chose Hindu names as their on-screen names. Just like Yusuf Khan was Dilip Kumar, soon Meher turned into Purnima. There was no going back after that. The film released a year after Independence in 1948, when she was just sixteen. It was only a matter of time before she was offered her first Hindi film, *Thes*, featuring Shashikala and Bharat Bhushan in primary roles. After that, she bagged a couple of other big films, *Narad Muni* and *Patanga*. While two of these three films were not hits, producer Bhagwan Dass Varma's *Patanga* proved to be very successful. She eventually married Bhagwan Dass Varma after her separation with Shaukat Hashmi.

Bhagwan Dass Varma was a famous producer–director of his time who had many successful films like *Patanga*, *Sagai*, *Badal*, *Aurat*, *Parvat* and *Pooja* under his banner of Varma Films. But he and my grandmother also faced a rough financial phase that many don't know of. She had become a guarantor of one Varma Films production that bombed so badly that they went bankrupt. My father told me that she owned a few imported cars, including a Buick. But she was not financially savvy, which led to her losing money to bad paperwork. The debt from the dud film was the last straw. She was very fond of her bungalow in Pali Hill that she had named after her niece—Heena. They were in such dire straits that the income tax department had to auction off the bungalow. With the money they got from selling the bungalow, they bought and moved into a much smaller flat in a building in Pali Hill itself—the house that I was born, brought up and still live in. As for the bungalow, it was bought by film-maker Vijay Anand and was rechristened 'Ketnav' and is a famous theatre and gallery now.

In spite of the size, the new flat was considered to be lucky for my grandmother though, as she got some very good character roles after we moved in. She also had great music in her films, with most of the hit songs picturized on her. Even back then, songs were an integral part of Hindi films and my grandmother was blessed to have celebrated artists like Lata Mangeshkar sing for her. We always joked that her luck of having good songs also seeped into my destiny, as my movies have great music too.

Bhagwan Dass Varma passed away in 1962. By then my grandmother was a respectable figure in the film circuit, and continued acting consistently. My father used to accompany her to the sets once in a while during his summer holidays but he never quite took to films. In fact, he had even acted in a film in 1968 called *Baharon Ki Manzil* opposite Farida Jalal after which he decided never to do another one. This was eleven years before I was born.

Growing up with my grandmother, I imbibed a lot of her characteristics. She was a strong-willed woman. It was probably in her genes, as her mother was like that too. My great-grandmother used to gamble and smoke, and would tell her daughters to elope with the men they loved if their families opposed the marriages! When my grandmother was pregnant with my father, her mother wanted her to deliver him in South Bombay's best hospital. They lacked the funds for such an expensive delivery, but my great-grandmother was adamant. So they did end up admitting her. After giving birth to my father, my grandmother was resting in her hospital bed late at night when my great-grandmother walked in gingerly and woke my grandmother up. What followed was bizarre. She sneaked out my heavily sedated grandmother and the baby from the hospital to avoid footing the steep bills! Bhatt Sahaab drew inspiration from this story and used it in our film *Hamari Adhuri Kahaani*.

I was very fond of my grandmother. She was the one who always encouraged me to take up acting and was the one who finally convinced me to do so. She had even enrolled me into acting classes when I was a kid. I still remember her proud smile when she saw my first TV commercial for Good Knight mosquito repellent—I was four then. Her dream to see me as an actor came true on 15 August 2003, the day *Footpath* was released.

She was very fond of Ayaan. She would cradle him in her arms and play with him for hours. But alas, their time together was short. In one of her last films directed by Bhatt Sahaab called *Naam*, she had played Sanjay Dutt's on-screen grandmother who suffered from Alzheimer's disease. Ironically, in 2010 she was diagnosed with Alzheimer's in real life as well. It was a traumatic phase for the entire family, to see her vaguely recall memories. Certain long-term memories were permanently etched in her mind while the more recent ones began to fade away. For instance, she clutched onto the fact that she was a film star, but she forgot who Ayaan was. And then, she forgot who I was too. It was like a videotape playing backwards, with her latest memories being erased first. It was a time of immeasurable despair for me, as I spent hours by her side trying to tell her who I was only to be met with blank stares, a few mumbled words and some weak shrugs. She had lost her motor skills by then and was permanently bedridden. Just like her memory, she was fading away . . .

It was 15 August 2013 when she breathed her last at Hinduja Hospital in Khar. She was surrounded by thirty of her family members. Each of us had fond memories of the times we spent with her. But alas, she did not recognize any of us as her eyes closed for the last time. I still remember the sound that accompanied the visual. It was the sound of the ECG machine beeping, till it flattened. I literally saw my grandmother fade away over the course of three hours. The sound still haunts me when I visit hospitals. Instead of mourning her demise though, we celebrated her life, a glorious journey. Here was a woman who had seen and withstood it all. She was a true star in every sense. It was a peaceful, painless passing. I had smiled to myself as a tear rolled down my cheek. I remembered vividly the same date a decade ago. *15 August 2003. The day* Footpath *had released.* She had passed away on the same day that I had completed ten years of being an actor. Such things can't be scripted.

SEVEN

CHEMO IN CANADA

'Stop fidgeting and keep the mask on!' I chided Ayaan, as he kept trying to pull off the mask that I had made him wear to cover his nose and mouth to prevent any germ intake. We were on our way to Toronto with a layover at Brussels. It was a long flight and the thought of Ayaan being in an enclosed space full of stale, canned air made someone as paranoid as me quite uncomfortable. I did not want him to breathe in the impurities and acquire an infection. I just did not want to take any chances even though the doctors back in Mumbai had said that it was okay for him not to wear a mask. He had just taken his first chemo a day ago, and I was fearful of an infection or anything that could throw a spanner in the wheels of the ensuing treatment. I didn't want any unwanted complications. But being the feisty kid that he is, he tugged it off again.

'Let it be,' Parveen intervened as I was about to pull it back onto his face. 'It's disturbing him. Besides, the doctor said it's fine.'

He handed her the mask, snuggled up to her and shot me a triumphant grin. I tried to frown back but ended up smiling meekly. It had been a tiring day. Just before we boarded the flight, we had a little adventure of our own. There was an important folder that had Ayaan's sonography results, medical papers, slides, chemotherapy details of the first session at Hinduja Hospital that we had to carry along with us to show the doctors in Toronto. Parveen thought I had packed it and I thought it was with her. It was a classic mix-up. Luckily enough, she asked me once we had checked in our luggage if I had the folder with the papers in our hand baggage. I was surprised and realized we had left it at home. Ayaan giggled looking at both of us getting worried over some silly plastic folder. I spoke to the airport officials who understood my situation and allowed me to wait it out until the papers were sent from home. It was a good thing we were at the airport way before the flight time, or else it would have been impossible to delay the flight or leave the country without those all-important documents.

All that running around and the recent events had left me physically and mentally spent. Despite that, every time I tried to rest my head, I couldn't relax and sleep evaded me completely.

I cast a sideways glance to see Ayaan nestled up in Parveen's arms, both of them sleeping peacefully. Seeing them in that tender moment, I patted both of their heads gently and played with their hair. I smiled tiredly at Parveen's mother, who was also travelling with us, seated across the aisle. This was my family, and whatever this little hurdle we had to face, we would overcome it together; it would never take us apart. I loved them and we would see this through, I promised myself. With that thought, my eyes closed for what seemed like a few seconds before the pilot's voice announced that we were about to touch base in Brussels. We had been airborne for a good nine hours.

At Brussels airport, Ayaan was awake and his chirpy self. With a spring in his step, he walked in front of us, excited to be in a foreign land. We asked him to slow down, worried about his weakness. But he shunned our pleas and continued to bounce away cheerfully. After about a minute, he slowed down, turned and looked up at me with wide, longing eyes. The kind he made when he wanted something.

'What is it, Ayaan?' I raised an eyebrow as I stood tall over him. He pointed at a Pizza Hut outlet a short distance away.

I looked at Parveen. She looked back at me. We had to tackle this smartly. In all my research on cancer I was shocked to learn that sugar feeds the disease. Processed food was also detrimental to the body causing it harm that was beyond repair. I had made up my mind that junk food like burgers, pizzas, soda pops and the whole lot of trashy stuff that kids love was going to be a strict no-no for Ayaan and the rest of us henceforth. I did not want to take any chances.

'Ayaan, come here.' Parveen took the initiative. 'Are you hungry?'

'Yes,' he muttered as Parveen lifted him up. 'I want pizza!'

'I'll get you something better than pizza.' I smiled. 'I'll just be back. Go sit there until then, all of you.'

As they left, I motioned Parveen to turn on her phone and activate her foreign card. She understood what I meant. I turned on my phone as well and walked towards the Pizza Hut outlet in case his eyes were following me. I took a sharp turn and stood in a corner, out of his line of sight before I made the call. I dialled Parveen's number and she answered after a few moments. I guess she showed Ayaan the Bat symbol flashing on her phone.

'H—hello?'

It was Parveen's voice this time. Without realizing, I continued in my Batman voice.

'Give the phone to Ayaan,' I growled. She chuckled first and then quickly covered up by telling Ayaan that a strange man had called and was asking for him. He knew who it was, of course. He grabbed the phone.

'Ayaan, it's Batman speaking,' I spoke. 'If Mama is around, take a few steps away from her so that she doesn't listen to us speak.'

'Yes,' he said. 'Yes, now we can talk.'

'You want to be a superhero, don't you? You want to be Ayaan Man, right?'

A few passers-by shot me quizzical looks, wondering why I was talking strangely into a phone.

'Yes, Batman! I want to be a superhero!'

'Then listen to me carefully,' I said. 'You are not going to have pizzas, burgers, French fries or any of that any more. None of us superheroes have that because it can make us unhealthy and fat. We lose our powers.'

He deliberated over the latest piece of information momentarily.

'Okay Ayaan? I will send you some good food.'

Still no answer. Quitting pizzas and burgers was going to be tough for him. For anyone, for that matter. It wasn't fair on him, to be honest. At his age, he was supposed to be enjoying junk food, desserts, sodas and a whole lot of things I had discovered to be extremely toxic.

'Okay,' he said meekly.

'Bye Ayaan,' I said. 'You'll be a superhero very soon!'

'Bye Batman,' he spoke in a resigned tone.

I returned after five minutes. I had searched for another store which sold some basic organic snacks and bought organic chocolate milk and some natural nutritional bars.

He took them from my hand, inspected them for a bit and then gobbled them up without revolting. He did not find the food bad, luckily enough. He couldn't afford to. This had to become a way of life for him and for us.

Soon, he was asleep in Parveen's arms as we waited to board the next flight. It was going to take another nine hours approximately, and I needed to catch up on some sleep before we landed. But at that moment it seemed impossible given the chaotic thoughts swirling through my mind.

I had literally tried every possible thing that could bring me comfort. Finally, I replayed Bhatt Sahaab's words in my head, telling me that Ayaan was a strong kid and that this was a minor hurdle that he would overcome in no time. And with that thought, I finally managed to doze off for a couple of hours.

It was January 2014 and Canada was experiencing one of its coldest winters that year. Our teeth began to chatter as we made an exit from the plane and walked into Ontario airport. Even though we were clad in thick jackets, we were still pretty unprepared to deal with temperatures as low as -35 degrees. After all we lived in Mumbai where any temperature a fraction below 20 degrees is considered to be winter. Toronto was a different ball game altogether. Our blood could've literally frozen in our veins. It was that frigid. We had mentally prepared ourselves for this kind of weather but we were worried about Ayaan. We did not want him to catch a cold, run a fever or get a chest congestion as this would mean that he would not be able to undergo chemotherapy. But Ayaan seemed to enjoy the new environment. Energized after the nap, he skipped away with his Angry Birds trolley in tow, as we collected our baggage and headed out of the airport.

My brother-in-law, Avinash Shahani, was to pick us up from the airport. He had been working in Canada for the past eight years and had settled there. As our eyes scanned the area to spot him, Ayaan beat us to it. He left his trolley abruptly and ran to his uncle with his arms outstretched. Avi bent down on one knee and hugged him. It was surprising to see Ayaan's familiarity with his uncle since he had only met him twice before when we visited his family in Canada. But Ayaan took to Avi right away.

'I thought he was unwell,' Avi took me aside and whispered as he embraced me warmly. He was briefed by Parveen to not bring up the ailment in front of Ayaan and keep the superhero story going. 'He seems like quite a happy kid.'

I smiled back as he led us to his car parked a short distance away. I lifted Ayaan up in my arms, lest he be tempted to pick up and play with the snow. It was the first time he had seen it and was fascinated.

'Look, Papa! There's snow!' he gasped, completely mesmerized. Eventually, he did manage to get a handful of it from the top of the car before we got in.

As we drove towards Avi's house, we tried to keep the mood light. We did not want to start talking about Ayaan's treatment in front of him just yet. Ayaan still had no inkling about the impending chemotherapy sessions. For him it was a holiday and we had to keep it that way. I looked out of the snow-laced window and saw hoardings that read, 'Tripped on your neighbour's ice? Call us now!'

'What's that?' I enquired.

'Well, it is exactly what it says,' Avi replied with a wry smile. 'If you slip on ice that your neighbours didn't care to clean out of their front yard, you can sue them. They're called slip-and-fall cases.'

I laughed out loud. Here we were in a country that allowed you to sue a neighbour if you tripped on some ice. And back home, you could get away with so much worse!

'I don't believe it,' I said, still laughing.

'Oh, wait till we get home.' Avi winked as we took a smooth turn into a lane and stopped outside his bungalow.

I pulled out the luggage from the trunk. Ayaan looked excited about running back to the room he had grown fond of during our last visit. 'It's been a long day. We should get some sleep. Then we can have some fun tomorrow,' I said.

And by that I meant we were going to take him to SickKids Hospital the next day.

I got up early the following morning. My body clock was still accustomed to Mumbai. I was used to exercising in the morning, but one look outside and I knew that there was no way I could go out for a jog. I stepped out of the room leaving Parveen and Ayaan who were still fast asleep to prepare some eggs and tea for myself. As I walked out, the little dog—Lico—came rushing towards me and began climbing up my leg, requesting frantically to be petted. I played with his soft black fur as it woofed away softly. Ayaan had really enjoyed Lico's company the night before. They had got along like a house on fire. Both of them were extremely friendly for their respective species. Except men change with age, dogs don't.

Avi greeted me as I went downstairs.

'You're up early,' he said, smiling.

'I usually wake up around this time in Mumbai too,' I replied. 'I work out. But doesn't look like that's going to happen here.'

I pushed the curtain aside to see a bed of snow covering the front yard and the road. The aftermath of a late-night blizzard.

Avi smirked. 'So you want to work out, huh?'

'Do you have something in mind? A treadmill at home, perhaps?'

'Something better,' he grinned and pointed out to the snow.

Within the next ten minutes, we were shovelling snow out of the front yard. The biting cold wind was stinging away at whatever skin that was exposed—my face was numb. But there was a certain thrill to it. And I'm sure it was gruelling exercise for a good half an hour. Soon enough, the driveway was clear of snow. What was left was two men whose teeth clattered and muscles ached. We went back in to see Ayaan and Parveen ready and dressed for the day. Ayaan was playing with Lico. Avi would drive us to SickKids that day. He stayed in Mississauga, which is an hour away from Downtown Toronto, where the hospital was located. Avi and I went to our respective rooms to change before we could head out to SickKids. Ayaan had no idea where we were going. He thought we were off to a mall and was thrilled with the idea.

The drive to SickKids was a slow one. A harsh blizzard had hit Toronto. The car windscreen was splattered with ice and snow.

Avi drove cautiously as any speed above a certain limit could make the vehicle skid. Ayaan enjoyed the ride though, fascinated as ever by the sea of snow. After a long drive, we finally halted outside the huge hospital located at the University Avenue.

Parveen, Ayaan and I gasped collectively as we looked up at the gigantic, well-designed hospital, which was partially glass and partially stone. Avi led us inside. He had taken the day off and was going to work at night in one of the hotels he managed.

Our first stop was at the International Patients' Department, where we met a Canadian-born Indian gentleman called Kenneth. He filled us in on the approximate cost of the treatment, the payment methods and schedules. The staff was extremely friendly and some of them recognized me. Bollywood films are quite the rage in Canada and the Indian staff who knew me had briefed the locals. We had quite a warm welcome in the IPD meeting room. After this procedural visit, we headed towards the main hospital, right across the road. It was a couple of minutes away and I carried Ayaan, who was safely wrapped up in a couple of sweaters.

As we entered, we realized that SickKids was nothing like what the name suggested, which was depressing and banal. Unlike the drab hospital that we had pictured, it was in fact something like a ten-storey mall! I had never even imagined that such a humongous facility could be a hospital for children. We were supposed to meet Dr Abha Gupta, one of the best at the institute, and someone that Dr Banavali from Tata Memorial Hospital had strongly recommended.

Ayaan was in a daze. There were toys everywhere. There were big posters of Mickey Mouse and other cartoon characters that were meant to put a smile on the kids' faces. They had the desired effect on Ayaan. He had no idea that this was a hospital even though I'm pretty sure he had registered a few doctors and staff in white hovering around. But I think his mind blocked them out and focused on the play area and the hundreds of toys that were in it. He tugged away at Parveen's dress, insisting to go and play. The play area was really alluring. *Hell, I wanted to go and play.*

'It's okay,' I told Parveen. 'It's better if you guys wait here. Let Ayaan play. I'll go and sort the other stuff out.'

Parveen agreed. I went and met the management, which included a couple of Indian guys too. There was tons of paperwork to take care of. They asked me all sorts of questions, including details regarding the payment of the treatment, the history of Ayaan's ailment and so on. After I spent a considerable time there, I was finally told that I could meet Dr Abha Gupta.

It was a task to get Ayaan out of the play area. We had to convince him that we were taking him to another one. That is when he reluctantly let go of a toy and trudged towards us. And we were right. There was another huge play area near the place where we had to go and wait for our next appointment. There were other parents waiting as well, so we had to join the queue. But till our turn came, we could submit our form to a gentleman who manned the play area. He would then talk to the kid and help him with the video games of his choice. This was, ironically, paradise for Ayaan!

We went into Dr Abha's cabin after a half-hour wait. She stood up as we entered and greeted us. She was a young lady with an affable smile that she directed towards Ayaan as soon as we walked in. The head nurse, Jill, trotted up to Ayaan right away and introduced herself. Her voice was squeaky, and she had long red hair. She seemed like a character right out of a Disney film. She was very animated, but Ayaan smelled trouble. This particular environ seemed familiar. He saw the stethoscope that lay on the side of the table and ran out of the room without another word. Before we could take off after him to get him back, Jill was already in pursuit of the little absconder.

'Don't worry,' Dr Abha said. 'Jill is good with kids. Give her a few minutes.'

And she knew what she was talking about. Jill came back holding Ayaan's hand. They were both giggling about something loudly and had certainly hit it off. I was already convinced that SickKids was a great choice. Abha took the slides and the other material from us and started studying them. After a couple of minutes, punctuated by Ayaan's laughter courtesy Jill, Abha looked up from the documents at us.

'So you guys have got the tumour removed, taken the first chemo and have flown him to Toronto within a week?' she said, completely amazed. 'You guys should be in the Guinness Book of World Records or something!'

Parveen and I looked at each other, then back at the doctor and just shrugged.

'In a place like Canada, by the time you get a bed or booking for a surgery it takes at least fifteen days! What you guys have done is unheard of!'

'Thankfully I was born in India,' I quipped.

'We are going to review the slides again ourselves.' Abha got down to business. 'As per your staging, it's stage two. But we will get back to you after three or four days. A week tops. You must understand that your pathology reports were done in Mumbai. We just want to redo and study the slides to be absolutely sure about the staging.'

Parveen and I were shaken. Our confidence took an unexpected blow. We feared that there was the possibility of something else cropping up. What if the staging was wrong?

'Don't worry,' Dr Abha said seeing our furrowed brows. 'This is routine procedure. It's great that you have detected it at the second stage. The problem arises when you detect it at the third or fourth stage. That's when you have to opt for radiation. In which case there is a strong possibility that the person won't be able to conceive and will be rendered infertile. A stage-three or stage-four kid needs check-ups even when they are forty and fifty, because the heart goes weak.'

I was a little shaken, I mean, I hated the fact that we detected a cancer at all, but I was relieved it wasn't too late.

'What I'm saying is,' Dr Abha continued, 'this is standard stuff. The timelines regarding the treatment remain somewhat the same for stage-one and stage-two cancer. The side effects aren't that dangerous. I mean, he'll lose his hair and throw up, but those side effects are routine . . .'

My face fell. I couldn't come to terms with the fact that Ayaan would lose his hair. It sent a shiver down my spine.

'I know what you're thinking,' she said. 'But trust me, you've got it easy in comparison to some other kids.'

And as if on cue, a little girl walked in along with a nurse who was as cheerful as Jill. Abha introduced us to her. She was shrivelled up, wafer-thin and had her head covered in a pink bandana. I also noticed that she didn't have eyebrows. I could feel a sudden weight on my chest. I could sense a phantom placing its hands on my neck and tightening its grip. I simply choked. I looked at Parveen, whose eyes had welled up. She in turn, looked at Dr Abha.

'The girl has leukaemia,' she mouthed softly. 'She's just eight.'

I sighed heavily. The girl's laughter resonated within the confines of the cabin as the nurse cracked her up. The sound of her laughing was both heartening and heartbreaking. Dr Abha was right. *We probably did have it easier.*

~

It was Tuesday, 29 January, when we came in next. Dr Abha had informed us about the procedures that were about to take place in our previous meeting. The first step leading to chemotherapy of this nature is a minor forty-five minute surgery for the insertion of a device known as a 'portacath' , or simply 'port'. Ayaan had already taken one dose of chemo in Mumbai without a port. But Dr Abha said that this was a better option, even though it entailed having to undergo a surgery.

In a nutshell, a 'port' is a plastic portal that is inserted in the chest beneath the skin and connected by a catheter to a vein. The chemotherapy drugs can then be injected into a septum of the port and it is more comfortable for the patient than administering it through the traditional IV. A port is usually installed into someone who has to undergo frequent chemotherapy. It is a safer way to inject the drug, so as to avoid the drug from spilling and searing the skin and muscle tissues. The primary usage, however, is to deliver the drug quickly and efficiently via the body's circulatory system. A catheter runs from the portal and is surgically inserted into a vein, which in Ayaan's case was the superior vena cava. This was a large vein in the right atrium of the heart that could then facilitate efficient pumping of the chemotherapy drug that the doctors decided was suitable. The other option, of course, was to administer the drugs intravenously through the arm. But it is a little dicey when it comes to kids, as they can accidentally tug on the tube and dislodge it. A port, on the other hand, helps avoid such situations and also spares the child the constant pain and trauma accompanied with intravenous injection. Ayaan, for one, had already developed a fear of being pricked by needles, because in Mumbai he was poked several times for the tests that we had had to conduct. So we agreed that the port was the best way out.

Before the operation, Parveen and I were made to sit with the doctor who told us about every possibility or complications that could arise. It was the standard protocol in many countries, where all the probabilities and outcomes of any surgical procedure were spelt out to the family of the patient, and only after their consent was taken, could the procedure be followed. At the end of this, we were supposed to sign a document that stated that we were made aware of all the possibilities. This standard procedure was followed to avoid legal redressals. The doctor opposite me began to rattle off all the side effects, possible snags and impediments. At the end of the list was the one thing we feared most—death—despite the chances being a minuscule 0.5 per cent. Needless to say, Parveen and I freaked out. We started questioning our decision to sit with the doctor at all for this particular conversation. And now that we knew that death was one of the probabilities, we were suddenly tormented by an unrelenting paranoia which would make this operation even more worrisome than the removal of the tumour itself!

Before the surgery, we needed to get Ayaan's blood pressure and a few other vitals tested. He was made to wear a hospital gown, similar to the one he wore in Mumbai. He felt betrayed and threw a fit, as he knew where all this was leading to. The poor kid had been through a lot already back in India, and he had no inkling about what the Canada trip was about. A sense of déjà vu struck him once he was wheeled into the hospital room. When we went in, I noticed that they had a great set-up. The first nurse walked in. Ayaan shrieked in fear the moment he saw her holding a syringe. He realized the ordeal hadn't ended. Parveen walked up to him and held him down. I was in the room with Avi, and I realized that he had probably not seen this coming. In the last few days, Ayaan had been through hell. He had had a surgery where he was cut across his midriff, he had had morphine injected into him, and got three injections (for testing his vitals and the first dose of chemotherapy).

'Is your husband okay?' the nurse addressed Parveen. They all looked at me amusedly.

Without realizing it, I had turned my back to them, and was rocking back and forth on my heels, clenching my teeth. I didn't have the stomach to deal with this and I couldn't even put on

a show any more. My wife showed more poise. I realized that
when it comes to emotional trauma, women are much stronger
than men.

'His blood pressure is really high,' the nurse gasped. 'It was
almost touching 180. It's probably the device's fault. It must be
spoilt.'

This didn't help my case. I was on the verge of a nervous
breakdown, because if his blood pressure was that high, there was
no question of the surgery happening immediately, and we would
lose days. She decided to do it again.

'It's 170 this time,' she said.

We understood why it was that high. Ayaan was so frantic
and hyper on seeing the nurse that his blood pressure peaked to
an unreal number. Parveen's voice had a way of calming Ayaan.
She knew distracting him would help immensely and promptly
handed him an iPad, on which we played an episode of *Mr Bean*.
It seemed to work as he laughed his guts out! We took a twenty-
minute break, and his blood pressure dropped to a normal range
the third time we tested him. Ayaan was pricked with the IV
needle once again, probably and hopefully for the last time, for
after this the medication was to go through the port. He screamed
at the top of his voice, and I couldn't look. I wanted to run out
of the room, but I had to pin him down because his constant
shaking was making the needle move under his skin and cause
more pain. Once the needle was in properly, he couldn't feel it
any more. After the procedure, he was ready to be wheeled into a
sterile room for the operation. Parveen, Avi and I waited outside
for a bit talking to a young nurse who I learned was an intern at
the hospital. She ensured us that Ayaan's treatment was not as
risky as some of the other cases that they dealt with. Our little chat
with her was heartening for us as parents.

Within forty-five minutes, the port was inserted under the
skin and above Ayaan's heart. While the surgery was being carried

out, Avi and I waited in the canteen, getting ourselves some quick sushi. We packed some and took it to Parveen in the waiting room who did not want to leave her place in case our names were called out. I even pulled out my diary and began to chalk out a revised schedule for my shoots. I had received a text from a representative at UTV Films a day ago, saying that they were willing to put *Raja Natwarlal* on hold indefinitely. I didn't want that to happen. I replied, telling him that I would manage to complete the film without having to push the release date. As Parveen ate, I pencilled down a new schedule to juggle my various commitments.

But I was distracted. The waiting room was flooded with parents like us. It was here that I realized how paediatric cancer had become a rampant malady. We were in the cancer ward on the eighth floor. I still remember walking down the passage. The cries of both parents and children still echo in my head when I think about it. The kids cried in revolt against the chemo while the parents cried seeing them in pain. There were kids all over being wheeled around on stretchers, some of them too weak to even keep their eyes open. The parents walked besides them with a glint of hope in their eyes, waiting for the bad dream to end.

A Canadian-born Indian man struck up a conversation with me. He had read about Ayaan's condition in the papers. He was a doctor himself and his son had a very rare form of retinal cancer.

'One day I just noticed a very unusual discoloration in my son's eye,' he spoke. 'I took him for a check-up and to my horror realized it was a form of retinal cancer. The eye had to be operated upon. We tried to save it, but couldn't.'

He wore a sad smile on his face.

'Well, at least he will be fine after this,' he continued. 'But don't worry, your son will be okay too. After reading about his case, I'm pretty certain of that. Children are extremely resilient. Their cells regenerate and renew at a rapid pace.'

I felt slightly encouraged. Every time someone said that Ayaan would be fine, it gave me the hope I desperately needed.

After the surgery, Ayaan was wheeled into another ward in a drugged state, sedated with anaesthesia, ready to get the vincristine into his system (unlike in Mumbai where dactinomycin was administered, vincristine was the first drug that SickKids chose to battle his cancer). He came back to his senses in thirty minutes, and just like the last time he had been operated upon, he had not eaten for the last twelve hours. This had to be done, because with anaesthetics, patients tend to bring up their food and vomit it out. We gave him only fluids before the sedative and a few biscuits that he nibbled on reluctantly. He was very quiet and looked extremely angry. He had realized that this was no vacation. He had been lied to again. But thank God for Rowan Atkinson and Steve Jobs. The episodes of *Mr Bean* on his iPad cheered him up again.

They finished administering the chemo through the port they had just installed in the next fifteen minutes. He did not even realize when this was done as there was no pricking this time around. After patching up the port, which was important to stop the plastic pipe from getting infected with bacteria, Ayaan was ready to get back home. If bacteria attacked the pipe, we would have to remove it and that would mean that he would have to undergo the rest of the sessions through the IV needles. We had to be cautious to spare him that trauma. He was groggy and nauseous, but I was glad with the proceedings at SickKids. But there were many more sessions to go in the coming months, and one could not anticipate what problems could crop up . . .

~

'Emmi! Where are you?'

I could hear Avi's voice scream out for me. I was busy with my new pastime—shovelling ice. I had already shovelled out all the ice from our own front yard, but I realized that it wasn't an adequate enough workout. I then crossed over to the neighbours' bungalow, had a word with them and told them that I'd clean up their front yard too. They were more than happy to let me do it.

'Look to your right!' I screamed back. 'Here, Avi!'

He looked surprised to see me toil away at the neighbours' front yard. He rushed up to me and got straight to the point.

'The arrangements are done,' he said. 'I spoke to the guy. He'll be here in an hour.'

'Good,' I replied, my face half-frozen. 'Let's wake Ayaan up and get him ready. This is going to be his best birthday, I'm sure!'

We went back into the house. It was Ayaan's birthday, 3 February. In the midst of the chaotic chemo, the poor boy had forgotten that his special day was coming up. We refrained from cake because of the high amount of sugar it contained, and birthday or not, I wasn't going to take any chances. We had a surprise in store for him though. Something he was definitely not prepared for, in a good way, for a change.

It was around five in the evening when the car pulled up. A man strode out of it with a large suitcase and after a few greetings and handshakes, Avi led him to the basement, while I went upstairs to get Ayaan. He was playing with Lico and was preparing for the party with his cousins who would be visiting later that evening. But there was one visitor he was not expecting. My phone buzzed and I hastily unlocked it to see a text from Avi that simply read, 'He's ready'.

'Ayaan, come down. Someone's here to meet you.'

'I want to play with Lico,' he protested. Lico too growled at me, unhappy at my proposition of stealing away his newest buddy.

'Just say "hi" and then you can play with Lico again.' I smiled. 'Come now!'

I led him by the hand down the staircase and into the hall. He stopped as he saw who stood before him. His mouth was agape, his eyes were wide with disbelief. It was . . . *Iron Man!*

Ayaan's reaction wasn't one of joy. It was of awe. He was transfixed for a few seconds. And when he did manage to react, he turned around and ran into the nearest room! It was a mixed bag of emotions for him to be standing right in front of his favourite character from the movies! I had to follow him into the room and drag him out of there. After a few initial moments of fear, Ayaan warmed up to Iron Man. They even enjoyed a game of foosball among many other games for the next half an hour. It was one of the most bizarre and thrilling moments for a kid obsessed with superheroes, I'm pretty certain.

'It's time for me to go. I have to fight the bad guys,' Iron Man explained to Ayaan as he got ready to leave. 'Happy Birthday, Ayaan Man!'

Ayaan laughed ecstatically and hugged Iron Man, before asking him, 'Will you come to meet me again?'

'Yes,' Iron Man replied. 'And I will get the other Avengers along too!'

After they bid goodbye, Parveen led a dazed Ayaan back upstairs. We told the man after he had changed out of his suit about Ayaan's condition. He was touched, almost moved to tears. He didn't take any money from us. As he was leaving he promised to get back with his other friends who ran this little business of dressing up as superheroes and attending children's parties. The pay wasn't much, but they enjoyed making children smile in whatever little way they could. It was moments and people like these that reinstated my faith in humanity.

Ayaan's birthday went well, with family and close friends who visited and showered him with all sorts of gifts, right from superhero costumes to remote-control cars. He was thrilled with the presents that had been couriered from back home too.

Two days later it was time for Ayaan's second round of chemo. I remember the drive to the hospital in bad weather amidst another blizzard. Ayaan had started showing some side effects, like severe nausea and the occasional vomiting, but the vincristine hadn't taken its toll entirely yet. His second round on 5 February too went pretty smoothly.

Another week passed way, and now the side effects began to raise their ugly head. There was still no hair loss, but Ayaan began to feel a pinprick-like sensation in his sleep and would wake up bawling. He would, from what he managed to explain, experience a very acute form of pins and needles for a good ten minutes. He would even experience foot-drop, that is, while walking his feet would suddenly go limp and he would lose sensation in the leg. This began to really affect me. I was accustomed to seeing my kid running around, and this restricted him. Luckily, he had cousins who would visit him and play with him without exerting him too much and that would keep him occupied.

I had to leave for Mumbai on 12 February, the day of his third chemo session. As usual, as if on cue, a blizzard hit Ontario. It had been three Wednesdays in a row that we had had to travel in adverse weather. This time, despite our ploy to distract him with an iPad, Ayaan knew where he was heading. He was beginning to anticipate the routine. Waking up at seven in the morning, wearing a shirt (which was a must, considering it's easier to unbutton it and access the port in comparison to a T-shirt) was all a part of the drill. SickKids was a place he wasn't too sure of. I mean, it had toys and video games and all of that but then they would also take him into a ward and give him medicines and stick tubes into him. And just that thought made him nauseous enough to throw up on the way. It was almost as though he could taste the medicine; his face contorted into a scowl. He began to cry.

That night, after his third session, I remember leaning over to him before he slept.

'Ayaan, I have forgotten something with the pilot of the plane. I am going to bring it back okay?'

He was reluctant to believe me at first. His scepticism was justified, of course. But I had to try and get him to believe me. He sensed that I was leaving for a longish term and he expressed his disapproval over it vehemently.

'Don't go, Papa!' he kept saying, repeatedly.

'I will be back soon, Ayaan. I promise,' I would reply with a heavy heart. 'I'll be back as soon as the pilot returns my things! He needs some documents so that we can extend our holiday in Toronto. I even need to bring some stuff from Mumbai for you . . .'

My voice trailed off. *I will be back soon.* And by that I meant three months at the very least. The guilt was unbearable.

After he slept, I remember Parveen suggesting that I stay on. It was a formidable task, having to go through a hurdle of this magnitude all by herself. I laud her for the courage and sheer strength she showed. But she also knew that it wasn't possible for me to pull out. The losses would amount to crores of rupees. We had had this discussion before. I kissed her goodbye and turned to leave with a lump in my throat. Seeing me leave, Ayaan got very upset. I picked him up and gave him a tight hug that lasted at least a minute. As I was reassuring him that I would come back soon, Ayaan said, 'Wait, don't go yet, Papa.' Ayaan darted to the living room shouting, 'I want to give you something.' Ayaan was soon back with a small box of his favourite crayons. 'This is for you.' Ayaan always did this when I travelled away from home for a long shooting schedule. Sometimes it was a small car, a robot at other times. Perhaps he wanted me to think of him whenever I saw his little gifts. I decided to keep that small box of crayons with me all through the three months that I was going to be away from him.

~

I remember readying myself for a shot for Vikram Bhatt's project—*Mr X*—two days after I had landed. I had called Parveen while I was in the vanity van. She updated me about everything. We made it a point to speak at least twice every day and also Skype whenever we could.

'Is everything all right?' I asked her as soon as she picked up the phone. 'Is Ayaan okay?'

'Um, yes Emmi,' she replied. 'Everything is okay . . .'

Her voice trailed away. I sensed a certain reluctance. She wasn't telling me something and my heart started racing with fear.

'Parveen, tell me! You don't sound okay. Is everything all right? Has something happened to Ayaan?'

She remained silent.

'Tell me, Parveen!' I said loudly. 'I'm getting worried here!'

She finally began to speak.

'Well, the night after you left, Ayaan's nose began to bleed.'

I was stunned into a silence. This wasn't good. Not good at all.

'A—And then?' I asked. 'Has it stopped now?'

'Yes, it has.'

'Why didn't you tell me about this earlier?' I asked her, agitatedly. 'You should've told me about this as soon as it happened!'

'Emmi, if I had told you about it, you would've taken the next flight back!'

I buried my head into my free hand and closed my eyes. She was right. She knew me too well.

'Besides,' she continued. 'It's just a side effect. I spoke to the doctors about it.'

There was a knock at my van. *It was time to give my shot.*

'Okay, Parveen. I have to go now. I'll call you back soon.'

I disconnected and slumped into my couch for a few seconds. *God, why is this happening to my kid?* I needed to escape. I needed a vent. And acting was that portal for me. With great resolve and renewed energy I stood up, walked out of the van and slammed the door shut behind me.

EIGHT

SOLACE IN CINEMA

I leaned back and let my head rest against the porcelain of the bathtub. I felt a tremor of rage travel through my chest, upwards towards my throat. I sensed the blood rush to my head. My heart thumped away furiously against my ribcage and my fists were tightly clenched. My eyes, when I opened them, burned. And finally, I let it all out. I screamed. I roared. I bellowed. It was bloodcurdling. It was what I needed to do to release all the angst that had been building up within me since we discovered that Ayaan had cancer. It was as if the pain had been contained within a dam. And now that the dam had broken, there was no stopping it. It was misery akin to a burning body being placed in a tub of ice. I continued to howl, letting the torrent of torment flow out.

'And . . . CUT! Superb shot, Emmi!' Vikram bellowed.

My body was numb. My throat ached once I finally stopped shouting. My hair stood on end. I climbed out of the tub of ice, put on a robe and walked silently towards a chair as the others present on the set continued to stare at me. I was shooting for *Mr X*. In the film, I play a cop named Raghu (again, after *Footpath*) who had been wronged and tricked into a death trap. I was supposedly dead, but actually not quite. I had just about made it to this abandoned warehouse with the help of a couple of friends who had put me into a bathtub full of ice to help heal my burns and I was screaming because of the unbearable pain. This was the exact shot that Vikram was filming. In the subsequent shot, the other actors in the scene were discussing radiation and the underhand malpractices of pharmaceutical companies which was all a part of the script. As I lay in the ice, with my skin tingling away, these words hit a sore point. I had heard terms like 'radiation' several times back in Canada, and here I was again hearing those dreadful words.

'You got the shot bang on!' Vikram said, as I put on a shirt and tried to dry my hair with a towel. 'It was almost as if you felt the pain physically!'

I didn't know how to explain it to him, but it was true. The anguish was real and that shout was the manifestation of the festering pain. *I felt every bit of that pain. That pain was real. That shout was genuine.*

Being in front of the camera was oddly therapeutic for me. I was at ease with myself when I stood before it, acting out scenes and giving shots. Ever since I had returned from Canada, I had got back to work with a vengeance. It was a crazy way of living for me. There were these hectic schedules peppered with still, passive moments where Ayaan was all I had on my mind. These moments punctuated the time I had between shots, the time I waited in the vanity van or the time when make-up was being applied to my face (for *Mr X* I had to undergo a three-hour procedure each day for about a week, where they applied prosthetics to my face to make it look like I had been scalded). But every time I was giving a shot, speaking a dialogue or acting out a scene, I was a different person. I was the character I was playing. I wasn't the man whose four-year-old son was fighting a grave battle. I was the person I was supposed to be in the film. During that phase I realized how privileged I was to be an actor. I would put on new personas, albeit for short periods. Being an actor was my refuge, my only escape.

Besides *Mr X,* I had two other films to shoot. There was *Raja Natwarlal* produced by UTV and *Hamari Adhuri Kahani* by Fox Star Studios and Vishesh Films. In addition to this, I also had a little bit to complete in terms of promotion and pre-release build up to *Ungli,* a film produced by Karan Johar's Dharma Productions. My plate was full. And though by now it was amply clear that my personal life was a bit messy, another grim truth was that professionally I was going through a slump. A rough patch as they say.

The time between 2008 and 2013 was the golden phase of my career, I believe. It had kicked off with *Jannat* where I played a punter for cricket matches. The film was fresh and had a great storyline, accompanied by beautiful music. It was a rage, an instant hit. That was followed by some of the films that shaped my career for the better, made money at the box office and were even applauded critically. *Once Upon a Time in Mumbai* saw me essay the role of a gangster making his way to the top and I was heaped with praise for it. Following this was *Murder 2*, a story independent of the first one but of a similar fabric, with bold content and a shocking story. Then of course was the film that swept the critics and audiences away, *The Dirty Picture.* It was an outstanding film all round. A great script, with Vidya Balan essaying the role of south Indian siren Silk Smitha. It was the definition of a good, offbeat commercial film. And as a follow-up to that, I did the sequel to *Jannat*, a police–gangster drama that fared well commercially. And then there was *Shanghai*, a more understated political drama in which my performance was critically acclaimed. Commercially too, I had the biggest hit of my career in 2012, with the horror–thriller *Raaz 3.* The film raked in 85 crore, the most any film of mine had ever made at the time of writing this. Besides, this was an era where the 100 crore club was not commonplace. So far, so good. And then came 2013 . . .

Whilst filming for *Mr X*, *Raja Natwarlal* and *Hamari Adhuri Kahani*, I was entirely aware of the fact that my last two films (in 2013) had completely gone off the mark in terms of the business they did and the box office collections they garnered. They were, to put it flatly, flops. I had decided to reinvent myself as an actor now that I had been acting for about ten years and consciously experimented to explore my versatility. When you do that, many films can flop, and I was prepared for it. And such a phase cannot pass with just one or two films. Perceptions do not change overnight. People will take time to accept the transition of a Serial Kisser into an invisible vigilante or a family man or a timeless romantic hero. Even a hard-hitting film like *Shanghai* did not do well commercially for that matter though I still maintain that I am proud of the film and my performance in it. I had put a lot of effort into the role, by going through various theatre workshops and reconstructing myself as an actor. I was dabbling in a new area of acting space, and it was tough for the audiences to accept 'Emraan Hashmi Version 2'.

The string of damp squibs started with *Ek Thi Daayan*. The film was definitely a fresh horror–thriller on paper. It wasn't the typical in-your-face horror movie. It was experimental, offbeat and worth a go. Or so it seemed. The film, sadly, didn't live up to expectations at the box office. Then came *Ghanchakkar*, an evolved, quirky comedy with Vidya Balan cast opposite me. It was a film laced with generous amounts of black humour and revolved around a heist and one of its perpetrators suddenly suffering from bouts of amnesia. I had grown my hair and built six-pack abs to play the amnesiac thief in this subtle comedy. But clearly, Indian audiences preferred the laugh-out-loud, slapstick variety. The collections of *Ghanchakkar* seemed like the only funny thing about the movie to some trade pundits. I still stand by the films though. These were experiments that went wrong, probably in a market that they weren't meant for. For example, *Ghanchakkar* had an open end that kept you guessing. It's a film-making device that is used quite often in Hollywood. But if you tried it in our Indian markets, as we learnt the hard way, you were headed towards failure.

By the time Ayaan was diagnosed with cancer, I had already delivered these two flops. I was seeking reprieve and hoping to salvage whatever it was that I had lost with my next three films. There was also Rensil D'Silva's *Ungli* that I had finished filming for before Ayaan's diagnosis. It was the kind of film that had everything working against it. For instance, one of our main actors, Sanjay Dutt, was going to go to jail. Besides that, there were hundreds of other setbacks. Towards the end, we had lost faith in the film as a finished product, because it had become somewhat dated and lost relevance. But I still wanted to see it through, and unlike the other actors in the film, I decided to allot time to promote it once they had locked in a release date. I am not the kind of person who could wash my hands off a film completely no matter what it's fate. I still stand by a *Ghanchakkar, Ek Thi Daayan* or even an *Ungli* for that matter, without letting the criticism affect me. I wouldn't say that I haven't done films that weren't good. But at the same time, I feel responsible for them.

I have always been an unconventional actor and I maintain that. My films haven't been over the top. They haven't been designed to make hundreds of crores each! I don't pay heed to those astronomical numbers at all. For me, I'm very clear when I read a script. I analyse the character that I'm about to play and the entire arc the story takes, and if I like it, I do it. There are no blurred lines, or calculations of business in my mind. For me, if I do a film that has been made at a budget of thirty crore and rakes in seventy, I think that is quite a feat and the film is a success. It's more about return on investment, than joining a three-figure club at the box office. That's my business mantra. But of course, the media is unkind to films, ripping them apart ruthlessly if they don't match their grand ideas of success.

The big question, however, is, what is the definition of a successful film? Money? Perception? Critical acclaim? You would be lucky if you manage to garner all three with a film. I strongly disagree with a myopic approach and perception that every film that rakes in three-digit numbers is a success. Especially, if that film has a high cost, it doesn't end up making money. It's not rocket science. But the public is fooled by full-page ads with the grossly inflated three-digit numbers. I'd rather do a film that makes me and my team proud and makes a good amount too. It is for this reason in most of my films we aspire to experiment with fairly novel concepts that are made in a fair budget without compromises.

It's also amazing how everyone is a closet director here. If your film doesn't do well, they jump onto the bandwagon and deconstruct things for you like they are all ace film-makers and they have figured it all out. It's easy to be an armchair critic. Try getting down in the arena and you'll realize how drastically things change. There are always so many variables. And things aren't as simple as they seem from the outside. Some uptight analyst, who has probably never seen what a hundred crores look like in reality, is ready to call your film a debacle and a flop. In fact, I have even stated that as an actor my job is to give my hundred per cent, and I can't always guarantee you a hit but I can bring a flop to the table quite easily. There is no set formula for a film, especially the kinds I dare to dabble in, to become a hit. I would be lying if I say that if a film I worked in fails it does not trouble me, especially earlier on in my career. There are certain insecurities that come with the business even though I am not one to show them or let them consume me. Because that is the worst thing that can happen to a star. The paranoia can gnaw away at you from within, and grow just like a cancer. I would mull morosely over a flop for a bit earlier on in my career, take the criticism as it came and just try and do better the next time. But after a point, I realized the best way to operate was to give my hundred per cent to a film and then detach myself. This saves me from getting demoralized if the film is a flop or becoming complacent if it is a hit. Flops make you fight and come back with a bang. I hold my failures closer to me than my successes. Failure is delayed success and success is delayed failure. I also don't do films that are designed to make money, which are out and out commercial, masala films. I do films with what I think are strong storylines; if the money has to follow, it will. When I had started out, personally, I made just a lakh on *Footpath*. As of now, I make more than hundred per cent of that. Growth is a gradual process, especially if you are experimentative with films. I'm hoping it clicks for me and I am certain at some point it will. It's just a matter of time. And as everyone knows, I have had a slow and steady climb.

After a lacklustre 2013, 2014 brought in a fresh tussle right from the word go in the form of Ayaan's tumour. As things stood at the point where I left my ailing son back in Canada, I knew for certain that I had to deliver a hit. It was long overdue. And I was working extremely hard to make it happen. The fate of these three films—*Raja Natwarlal*, *Mr X* and *Hamari Adhuri Kahani*— of course, is something you might already know as you read this. I will get into greater detail about them a little later, and with good reason. Because as I was toiling away with work on these three, my son was fighting a battle of his own that made every other problem seem minuscule. And as difficult as it may have seemed for me to deliver a hit film, there was a more pressing issue out there. For if a film flops you might just bounce back with the next one. But with cancer, there were no second chances.

NINE

PARANOIA TAKES ITS TOLL

I had an important shot to give. Funnily enough, I didn't know what time of the day it was. I had to put on a suit and I was yet to get my make-up and hair done. My hands trembled violently as I switched on the light bulbs that were attached to the mirror in my vanity van. The yellowish light bounced off my gaunt face, as I saw my reflection. I was white as paper. More frail than usual. I proceeded to remove my T-shirt. My bare body was feeble, almost skeletal. And then, I spotted a bump under my ribcage. My eyes widened with horror. And then, I spotted another lump somewhere near the solar plexus. My shaky hands ran over it. The lump hardened defiantly beneath my fingertips, throbbing slowly at first and then pulsating rapidly. As my jaw dropped, I saw another large lump, almost the size of a tennis ball, over the area where my liver was supposed to be. And then, they all began to protrude causing my body to lose shape, almost like an amoeba. I saw my face in the mirror, about to let out a shriek. And just before I could, I woke up.

It was yet another nightmare about a tumour that had caused me to wake up in the middle of the night. The nightmares had started in Canada and continued in Mumbai. I had begun to experience abstract dreams about tumours quite regularly now.

Sometimes they were slightly more graphic, and I would literally feel them fester within me right until the point I would wake up with a start. I looked at the clock on the table next to my bed. It was four-thirty in the morning. I was sleep deprived and whenever I did manage to steal a few hours of sleep, my subconscious mind would start playing games with me. The insomnia and sleep deprivation had become such a problem that it began to show on my face. My make-up artist had a tough time concealing the dark circles. I even began to pop some sleeping pills every night in an effort to get those much coveted hours of sleep. I used to be groggy most of the time except when I would have to face the camera. That was when a new energy would sweep over me and I would feel fresh as ever.

As I slipped out of bed, I switched on the light and walked up to the mirror to take a look at myself. I checked my stomach to be doubly sure that my nightmare hadn't materialized in reality. The level of paranoia were unreal. I needed some fresh air. I just walked up to my drawer, pulled out the keys to my sports bike and decided to zoom around the city. Just like that, in my crumpled T-shirt and pyjamas, I took the lift to the ground floor, got on my bike and whizzed past my sleeping nightwatchman. The purring of the engine helped me escape to another space for about forty minutes, until my longish detour ended at Bandstand. I got off the bike and walked towards the sea, letting the salty breeze hit my face. The misty wind was like a soothing balm. The promenade was empty, save for a drunkard who would've sworn that he had seen Emraan Hashmi the next morning. My mind shifted back to the Skype video chat that I had had with Parveen earlier that night. As for Ayaan, we still hadn't had much of a conversation.

'Ayaan, please talk to me!' I pleaded, as he stared back at me over a bowl of breakfast cereal kept before him. 'I know you're upset, but the pilot trapped me and brought me back to Mumbai!'

He looked at me questioningly.

'Then why didn't you take another plane and come back?'

'Because I did not get a ticket,' I said. 'But I am going to get you some gifts when I return. Really!'

'I want you back here, Papa. Not the gifts.'

My heart sank again as those words reverberated in my head. I closed my eyes and rubbed my face with my hands. Ayaan had held a grouse against me ever since I had left him in Canada. It had been a few weeks already and I still tried to sell him the lie about the evil pilot and how he had trapped me in the plane and had brought me back to India. I would look at him and already see glimpses of what the chemotherapy was beginning to do to him. He still had a full head of hair, but there was something different about him. He had lost weight, Parveen had mentioned as she updated me about every little detail of his sessions and how they spent their day. The distance between us was painful. But I had to deal with it. For some more time at least. I lifted my head. The sky was brightening and the sun was about to rise. I stood up tiredly and got back to my bike. I had to be on a gruelling shoot schedule later that day. Instead of getting a good night's rest, here I was zooming around town in a helplessly insomniac state in the wee hours of the morning.

I went back to my room after parking my bike and passing by the nightwatchman who was still blissfully asleep. I envied him. I looked at that bottle of sleeping pills that rested on the table and considered taking one to steal a few hours of sleep before I would need to report at the set. After mulling over it for a few moments, I decided to just lie down and try to organically rest my body. Besides, I did not want to risk oversleeping. The shoots for both films, *Mr X* and *Raja Natwarlal*, were progressing smoothly and I didn't want to hamper that. I wanted to wrap them up quickly and head back to Toronto.

~

Time passed by between my hectic shooting schedules and erratic sleep routine. I had become somewhat of a recluse back in Mumbai and all I did was plug in my Apple TV and binge-watch television shows and movies. Ironically, I was addicted to the brilliant and gripping show *Breaking Bad* in which the protagonist Walter White is an ordinary high-school chemistry teacher who is diagnosed with lung cancer and then goes on a violent spree to secure his family's future before he dies. Ironic as it may seem, even my sources of entertainment had the element of cancer attached to them somehow. It was a lot like the Blue Car Syndrome!

Around a week later, I had to shoot for a sequence that required me to pull out a gun and fire. After giving the shot and a couple of retakes, I started getting a weird sensation in the left side of my chest and left arm. It felt as though a current of cold water gushed through my veins. I felt numb and I took a few moments off. The crew realized that something was amiss and called the doctor on the set.

'I hope this is not the onset of a chronic problem,' I voiced my concerns to Dr Agarwal. 'Especially since it's happening on the left side of the body.'

The doctor, after a few basic check-ups, realized the reason behind the problem.

'This is because of high stress. It's a clear indication of that,' he said. 'It's because of lack of sleep and the anxiety and tension that you have gone through over the past month. This is just a manifestation of that.'

He suggested a few medicines, which included a prescription for stronger sleeping pills.

'Don't worry about it,' he continued. 'Just sleep it out. You're overworked and mentally spent, and understandably so, because you have been through a tough time. This is a stress-related problem.'

I realized that I needed to take his advice seriously. My body was in severe need of sleep. I was literally working like a robot, functioning like clockwork. The only time of the day I felt alive was when I spoke to Parveen and Ayaan each night over Skype. It would be night in Mumbai and morning in Toronto, and they would call me up when it was time for breakfast. I would look forward to the nights, when I would come back home and talk to them. The distinct Skype ringtone was music to my ears.

'Hey Ayaan!' I would say cheerfully. 'How are you?'

He would just look at me, wave and then look away at the cartoons on the television screen. He was disinterested. He didn't want to interact with me more than he was forced to. He was angry and made no bones about it. In many ways, he is just like me.

'Emmi, his chemo is tomorrow,' Parveen said in a hushed tone, after moving out of Ayaan's earshot. 'Everyone loves him at the hospital, he's become quite popular. He's the most friendly kid they've seen! He kicks up a storm prior to the chemo but once it's done he just walks away smiling bravely.'

The image she created of my affable son made me smile. I could picture him strutting away, waving and smiling at the nurses as if nothing had happened.

'What about the side effects?' I asked.

'His pillow has more than a few strands of hair now,' she spoke. 'His hair is limp and scanty. It's really frightening, Emmi!'

The idea of my son losing his hair still sent shivers down my spine even though I knew that this was one of the most inevitable as well as harmless of the side effects.

'Yes, but we knew it's going to happen. Anything else?'

'Every time they administer dactinomycin he throws up 10–15 times in the next twenty-four hours,' she said. 'He's losing weight and he's having difficulty passing stools. But as of now, it's all under control.'

All these were indications of the chemo kicking in and doing its job. Even though it was worrying, such things were bound to happen. For instance, the drugs were known to act in a way that dropped the body fluid levels by a notch, which in turn made it harder to pass stools. Parveen kept Ayaan well hydrated with water, juices and healthy drinks, but she had to resort to laxatives for the bowel movements. And this was absolutely necessary, because if the kid was constipated or ran a high fever, he would not be in a position to undergo the chemo procedure, which would make us lose another week. This was a chance I was simply not willing to take. I wanted his chemo sessions to go as scheduled. God forbid, if he missed one, and everything went haywire, I would never be able to forgive myself for my negligence, I thought.

'Come on, Ayaan.' Parveen then turned her attention to him, as I watched it happen on my computer screen. 'Let's get ready! Mama will take you to Chuck E. Cheese!'

Chuck E. Cheese is this huge chain of restaurants for kids, with a friendly looking mouse as it's mascot. Ayaan found heaven in that place. It had video games and all sorts of stuff to keep him amused. It was a great escape for him. My only escape, on the other hand, was my shooting schedule. In fact, even on the night before my birthday I had occupied myself with shooting. I wasn't someone who believed in celebrating birthdays on a grand scale anyway. I usually had these small dinners with Parveen, Ayaan and a few close friends. But they weren't here and I did not feel like doing a thing without them. I just retired to my bedroom that night after a few hours of shooting. I hadn't called or responded to any of my friends' texts because I wanted to be left alone ever since I had got back from Toronto. But a few of my friends dropped by to cheer me up at ten and waited until the clock struck twelve, so that they could wish me!

They chided me. 'Why are you so disinterested, Emmi? It's your birthday in a couple of hours! You can't avoid treating us, you miser! Come on, we're going for dinner.'

'You know how it is, guys,' I replied with a sour smile.

They realized that I wasn't in the mood to go out and party.

'Do you want to do something at home itself, Emmi? We could call for dinner!'

My friends were trying hard to make my birthday as special as they could. I realized I shouldn't be playing spoilsport and should be thankful for having them around. In fact, even now, my best friends are the people I met in school or college, way before I entered this industry.

'Actually,' I smiled, 'let's all go out! Let me take you guys for dinner!'

So we did end up going out. That night out was a breath of fresh air. I hadn't laughed and spoken to my friends that way ever since the diagnosis. This little break was definitely necessary for me in more ways than one. I remember sleeping well that night and waking up in a much better frame of mind. Since it was my birthday, the shooting hours were shorter. I rushed back home after packing up, only to find a couple of missed calls on Skype from Parveen. After wishing me quickly for my birthday, Ayaan ran away to play. Parveen wore a look of anguish.

'Emmi, they want to do a blood transfusion for Ayaan,' she said urgently, her face strewn with worry. 'The platelet count has dropped drastically to four!'

I was petrified. Transfusion was one of those things that I had an inexplicable mental block against, especially if Ayaan had to undergo one. I called up a couple of doctors immediately while Parveen watched me on Skype and explained the situation. They told me that a transfusion was necessary only if the kid was feeling weak.

'Ayaan doesn't seem weak,' Parveen said right away when I told her this. 'His haemoglobin is low, but he's certainly not weak. He's chasing Lico all around the house right now!'

That bit of information provided me with some relief. I wanted to do anything to avoid the transfusion. I needed to make sure that his haemoglobin went back up within a week, or else it would leave us with no other option. I consulted my old friend—Google.

'Don't worry,' I replied. 'We'll get his haemoglobin back on track before the next round of chemo.'

In a couple of days, I was due to leave for South Africa. I had a schedule for *Raja Natwarlal* and a few portions of *Mr X* to shoot in Cape Town. I promised myself to find everything that I could to fix this new problem. I jotted down options to get his platelet count back to normal. I also learnt that the chemotherapy drugs probably had a role to play, as they were known to reduce the production of platelets. Among the quick-fix remedies that I discovered, a few included basic ingredients that were probably a part of everyone's kitchen. Broccoli, spinach, beetroot, papaya and even Vitamin C tablets were all good for the production of platelets. I kept sending Parveen texts informing her about my latest discoveries. She, in turn, kept giving Ayaan juices with these ingredients. He would throw tantrums sometimes, but that is when Batman chipped in.

Around a week later, when I had already gotten into the groove of filming *Raja Natwarlal* in Cape Town, I got a call from Parveen on set.

'His haemoglobin is back on track! It has shot up to 9!'

I excused myself from the set and walked into a secluded room. I was extremely happy, now that we had dodged the transfusion bullet.

'The people back at the hospital were amazed,' Parveen said with a chuckle. 'They actually took me and Ayaan to the dietician and asked me what I gave him to make his platelets go up like that. They were surprised that we took it up by such a margin in just a week!'

Well, by now I had learnt one thing about the net for sure. The Internet is a treasure trove with its unending plethora of information.

The Cape Town days were a lot more relaxed. Knowing myself, I was aware that if I went into a bad mood, it would be very difficult for me to work. I sought solace in humour and the general environment was far more relaxing. In Cape Town, by far my favourite destination, I would be really busy and would go out after shoots with my friends Kunal and Sonali. In fact, Anurag Basu had come down to Cape Town for the recce of his new film. He informed me that he had been cancer-free for the past ten years and that Ayaan would recover soon after the chemo. That was a major relief!

The third of May was drawing closer, and with that, the end of my schedule in Cape Town. But there was a new roadblock between me and Toronto. It was the imminent release of Rensil D'Silva's vigilante drama—*Ungli*. There were talks doing the rounds at producer Karan Johar's office of releasing the film in the middle of May. For me, that only meant one thing. I couldn't head back to Toronto to my family. I would have to be present for the various phases of promotion for the film. Some of the actors had backed out of promoting it and Sanjay Dutt was serving his jail sentence. That left only me, so I needed to see the film through to its release. I just hoped and prayed that the film's release would get postponed, otherwise I would have to be in India until the end of May.

And then it happened. My prayers were answered, as I woke up early to work out one morning in Cape Town. I got a call from Karan Johar's office saying that the film release was postponed to the second half of 2014. I was ecstatic! I was going to see Ayaan soon. And of course, Parveen. The backbone of my family. The love of my life.

With Parveen and her family on her birthday!

Parveen's birthday cake!

An outing in Toronto

Sunday by Snug Harbour,
Ontario Lake

The mandatory family snap!

As you can see, Ayaan loves
his ice cream

Just another part of me

Walking through the Blue Mountain woods

A trip to Paris

Ayaan with his cousin once he
came back to Mumbai

Homecoming!

Back to school!

Back to normalcy, on the road to recovery in Mumbai!

Ayaan Man!

Like father, like son

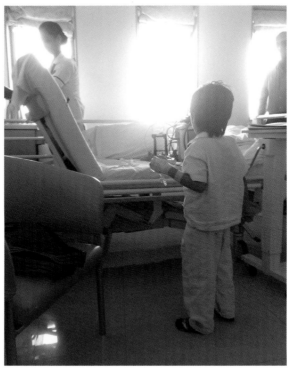

The first steps after the tumour removal at Hinduja
Hospital

Ayaan loves his Lego!

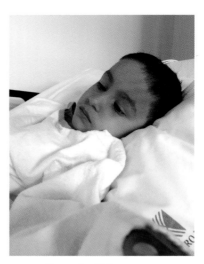

Sapped of his energy,
Ayaan rests for a bit

Iron Man and Ayaan Man!

Ayaan—mama's boy

The little league of superheroes!

Hold on tight, little one!

The first Diwali after Ayaan's treatment!

Ayaan with my dad,
Anwar Hashmi

Ayaan at the Golden Temple

TEN

THE ONLY ROMANCE
THAT MATTERS

'So Parveen,' I said, as I closed the rickety lift door behind us. 'What do you think about us?'

I punched the button to the floor I stayed on. We had organized a small casual get-together at my place with our college friends. I didn't have much time to get my answer, but now that I had asked her, I was waiting for a reply. I tried hard to avoid eye contact for the first few moments and to sound as nonchalant as possible. Maybe the lift isn't a great place to ask someone out after all.

'What do you mean, Emmi?'

I turned around to see her confused face.

'I like you,' I continued. My face was passive and didn't betray any emotion. She remained silent, trying to fully understand the import of what I was saying. I was surprisingly articulate despite being a little nervous.

'Should we start dating? I mean, I really like you.'

I was to the point and hoped it would work in my favour.

'This is not how it's done, Emraan.'

The lift stopped abruptly outside my flat. I was hoping I had a little more time. Our friends were waiting at my place and I knew we couldn't continue this topic in front of them.

'This is not how it's done,' she repeated. 'I'm not interested.'

Oops. I did not know how to react right away. She may have thought that I wasn't heartbroken and maybe I wasn't. But to be honest it did pinch a little. I was thinking of what to say next. Instead, I pushed the lift door open and let her walk out.

'Well, we'll see how it goes,' I said plainly.

And as it happened, Parveen Shahani did eventually get married to me. The persistence (and not the filmy kind) did pay off!

I had first met her through some mutual college buddies in the eleventh grade, in 1995. I was in Sydenham College and she was in HR College a few lanes away. We began to hang out as a group in Bandra. I learnt that she stayed two minutes away from my place. We began to meet quite often and hang around aimlessly on Carter Road. All of us would go to watch films to Sterling Theatre and Eros Theatre in South Mumbai. We would even frequent clubs such as Athena and Lush, which were a rage back then in the nineties. Pali Hill used to be quite a crazy place during the nights as a lot of college kids would get into their fathers' cars and zoom around with blaring music. Various groups had spots marked out for themselves, where they would gather and blast songs. We were no different. As a group, we even headed to Goa for trance festivals. That was the kind of music I always fancied and still listen to, quite a contrast to the Bollywood chartbusters in my films! I still remember what she had worn the first time I had seen her. We had gone to Prithvi Theatre for a play and there she was, wearing a dark shirt with white dungarees. Once we became friends, all of us hung out together for a good four years. Those were the carefree days! Parveen still teases me on how I stalked her and remembers the littlest details. Well, I didn't do it knowingly!

Once college ended, Parveen flew off to the United States to work and gain some job experience. I knew I'd miss her, even if not in the crestfallen manner of the characters I portrayed on celluloid. But I moved on, so to speak. I got busy with my work and she got busy with hers. We went our separate ways. For a short while.

Parveen returned from the States after six months. We hadn't met in a long while, but when we did, thanks to our mutual friends, we hit it off instantly. Making up for lost time, we began to tell each other what we had been up to, how we were both caught up in making a career. I wasn't an actor just yet. By that time, however, I was pretty sure about my feelings for Parveen. And that is when I decided to put them forth in the lift that evening. It never really became awkward though. I knew she liked me too. We used to hang around often with friends and the two of us used to chat away just like in the good old college days. I would call her up at night when our respective families would be asleep, and we would talk for hours. I hadn't found that level of comfort with any other girl before. Parveen accepted me for who I was and she was the first girl around whom I could truly be myself. Eventually, we did start dating.

In 2004, I learnt that her mother was considering a Sindhi boy, who had asked for her hand in marriage. The match had come via a relative or something like that—you know how arranged marriages work. Anyway, things were getting pretty serious in the family with that match but I did not take it too seriously. What I knew from Parveen was that her mother would not approve of her having a relationship. For her it was an open-and-shut case—Sindhi guy; same community; arranged marriage; mother approves. Emraan? Not same community or religion? Love marriage? Not a chance!

In her defence though, I did not commit to anything more than just dating at that point. My film *Murder* was a hit, but I followed that up with a flop. My career was still at a shaky point and I did not want to get distracted by the prospect of marriage just yet. Probably I was just being like most guys at that age, scared of the responsibilities and changes that marriage would bring along. Understandably, she did not want to be with someone who wasn't willing to commit to something concrete. She loved me, but it wasn't a practical option. As a result, Parveen decided to go ahead and give her consent to the arranged marriage proposal. It was fixed.

I still remember the night when the news hit me and I realized the gravity of the situation for the first time. A bunch of us had made an impromptu plan and had gone for dinner to a restaurant, Papa Pancho, in Pali Hill. As we took our seats and began to order appetizers, Parveen got a phone call from the man she was about to marry. She began muttering something into the phone, and I couldn't exactly hear her. Her voice was drowned by the guffaws of my cheering friends. I watched her speak to him for a good five minutes. It ruffled my feathers. That was a wake-up call for me. *Quite literally.* The girl I was in love with was about to get married. What was I thinking? Was I really going to do nothing about it?

That night I pondered over our relationship quite a bit. I suddenly realized that Parveen meant more to me than my career. I needed to do something and I needed to do it fast. I decided to make my move the next day itself. We had planned another dinner, this time at a Chinese restaurant in Bandra. As dinner proceeded, I kept recalling the night before, when the guy had called her up. I cleared my throat. All my friends, Parveen included, looked at me.

'Guys,' I said, with an air of nonchalance as I looked directly at Parveen. 'What do you think about me and Parveen getting married?'

There was a pregnant pause. Everyone shot each other confused glances. I held Parveen's gaze. Her eyes were wide with disbelief. And then, everyone burst out laughing. They thought I was kidding. My face remained unchanged.

'I'm serious, guys.'

That cut short their guffaws.

One of them said, 'Well, if you are, this is certainly not how it's done, Emmi!'

'Not how it's done,' the others echoed, collectively.

But that is exactly how I did it. It took a while for Parveen to let it sink in. Only after mulling over it for a bit did she tell her mother, who opposed the idea, as expected. Eventually she did come around. Parveen's father had passed away when she was in the ninth grade, and ever since, it was her mother who had brought her up and taken care of her single-handedly. Needless to say, Parveen did not want to disobey her. But she succeeded in convincing her. Besides, I was also an actor with a promising career. Probably that was a factor that helped me get an edge over the other guy. But at the same time, I wasn't just any other actor. I was Emraan Hashmi, the man who had single-handedly corrupted the innocent nation with a film like *Murder*. So imagine how hard it would've been for an orthodox Sindhi household to digest the news that their daughter wanted to marry that guy. I mean accepting the promiscuous side of a character on screen is easy, but what if that actor really has that side to him? Eventually they did understand that it wasn't how it appeared. But it did take some coaxing on my part for them to agree. Meanwhile, the other guy who was all prepared to get married to Parveen, was certainly in for a rude shock. The scenario was reminiscent of *Dilwale Dulhaniya Le Jaayenge* minus the drama and the train sequence.

Parveen and I got engaged at her place. And after a while, we got married on 14 December 2006. Our courtship phase, right from the time I first asked her out to the day I married her, lasted about four years. From a time when I didn't have a penny in my pocket, as my father was from a middle-class background, to the point I became a successful movie star, Parveen continued to love me for who I was. She was there for me through each phase, and

I guess that's what got us closer. The intimacy with her was at an emotional level.

Of course, we have had a few tiffs regarding my films. Especially in the earlier years. It was a very natural way to react. I mean, had the roles been reversed, I would've thrown a fit myself to have my girlfriend or wife kiss attractive men as part of her job as an actress. I even remember on one occasion during the phase we were dating, where I showed Parveen the trailer of *Murder*, way before we got married. She saw a bit of it with a smile which soon disappeared. Her eyes widened in horror, as she saw me in character, unzipping my heroine's jeans and taking her top off.

'This is it,' she exclaimed, without even waiting to complete watching the trailer. 'I'm out of here!'

It took a great deal of convincing to talk her out of the bad mood. After our marriage, before I would shoot for a kissing scene, I remember calling my directors up, right from Anurag Basu to Kunal Deshmukh, to get them to talk to her.

'It's all very technical,' they would pacify her. 'Parveen, you need to calm down! Yes, it's just like "Emmi, look to your left!", "Tilt your head a bit!" It's all very mechanical, Parveen, trust us! There are hundreds of people on the set! It's just another shot.'

'It's not what it looks like,' I would add. 'It's definitely not fun! It's all just acting, believe me!'

And then she would concede reluctantly. In fact, when I was shooting for *Murder* I had deliberately not informed her about the erotic content in the film because she would've protested. When I was in Bangkok shooting for the film, I bought her gifts with my own money. I remember calling her from the store.

'Hey Parveen,' I said. 'There are a few pretty bags here. Should I bring one for you?'

'Which brand?' she asked right away.

I looked at one of the bags closely and read the name.

'Fendi,' I said nonchalantly. 'Should I get it?'

She let out an excited gasp. Apparently it was a big deal. I had no clue about brands, especially of women's handbags.

'I'll take that as a yes,' I laughed. 'In fact, I'll bring you two!'

Once I returned, we discovered that they were really accurate imitations of the original ones. We laughed a great deal at it then. She still brought up this episode now and again after we got married. Taking a cue from that first time, we even formed a pact. For every time I had to kiss my co-star on screen, I would need to buy her a gift. And if it was a Fendi or Louis Vuitton bag, I would have to accompany her to the store so that she could pick one. *Or else, you will turn up with counterfeits again.* Every kiss on screen was accompanied with a hefty price tag.

In fact, Parveen's favourite films among the ones I have acted in are the ones in which I haven't kissed. At every premiere that I would take her to, she would dig her nails deep into my hands whenever an intimate scene would come up. It was a tight, unforgiving clasp. The only films that my hands were spared in, were the ones without kissing scenes like *Shanghai* and *Once Upon a Time in Mumbai.* She kept praying that the Serial Kisser tag would leave me with time, but that didn't seem to happen. I would tell her that the films I didn't kissed in usually flopped. She understood, but it's still difficult for a wife to see her husband kissing another woman, even if it is just acting. I can only imagine how tough it was and still is for her.

On 3 February 2010, we were blessed with a little angel. A baby boy we named Ayaan. He consumed all our attention. He was and continues to be the focus of our lives. He is the best thing to have happened to us.

~

'So they were right there and they refused to meet you?' I asked my father, my temper rising.

'Yes,' he said solemnly. 'I waited there for quite a while. And then they sent a message through the broker saying that they didn't want to meet me.'

I was infuriated. I hated the idea of my father being disrespected in such a manner. *You can act tough with me, but don't you dare try it with my parents.* It was in 2009, and I had decided to invest in a flat. Parveen was pregnant at the time and I was either tending to her or shooting for a film. So my parents had decided to go and speak to the society themselves, since my plate was full. But when I returned home, my father relayed the incident to me. He had gone to get a No Objection Certificate for a flat that I had finalized in a building. The building was a cooperative housing society in Pali Hill. The society members were in a meeting and they made him wait for a long time. After which, they flatly refused to meet him. At that very moment, Bhatt Sahaab happened to call. He could sense the anger in my tone.

'What happened, Emmi?' he said mockingly. 'Angry with me?'

I went on to explain what had happened. And then he suggested that I speak to the Minorities Commission, because we felt that it was clearly a matter of discrimination on the basis of religion. As soon as I spoke to the man in charge, the media got wind of it. Which in turn meant that they had got enough fodder to fuel their yellow journalistic agendas for the rest of the month. Soon, it snowballed into a major issue with hundreds of legal and other ramifications. There was a huge uproar against us and people protested saying that our accusations were baseless. It wasn't just about the flat any more.

We backed out, not willing to get too deep into the matter. To hell with the damn flat. Parveen and my grandmother were quite worried about my well-being, considering the aftermath. In fact, a political party had even turned up below my residence and kicked up a ruckus with a protest. They accused me of disrupting the communal harmony of the area! The irony and hypocrisy of the situation did not escape me since such parties would go to any length to garner a healthy vote bank, and they were accusing me of disrupting harmony!

I bring up this incident here to explain my views on religion and how we have chosen to bring Ayaan up. My father is a devout Muslim. And by that I mean he prays five times a day and adheres to every Islamic rule. My mother is a Christian who converted primarily for practical purposes to marry my father and changed her name from Mavis to Maherah. She still worships Christ and there's no interference from my dad's side. I am born a Muslim, but the rest of my family is primarily Hindu. I have imbibed the best from all religions and am sensitive to every religion, its rules and viewpoints. When Parveen married me, we had a traditional nikah. She too still practises Hinduism and has built a temple in our house. I have never had a problem with that. My family is an amalgamation of many religious. I strongly doubt if there is a family as cosmopolitan as ours in the vicinity.

Therefore, when this incident happened, I was rudely shocked. I had never faced a problem of this nature before. My surprise was greater that it had happened in a tolerant city like Mumbai, especially in a locality like Pali Hill where I had expected people to respect the secular fabric that the country advocated so strongly. And this goes both ways—there is discrimination even in Muslim areas against Hindus. It's just one of the problems that doesn't look like it's going to get solved any time soon, even if the intent is there.

Regardless of what happened after that, I knew one thing for certain. I was sure of how I wanted to bring up Ayaan. I wanted to sculpt his mindset and outlook towards religion very early on. Personally, I am not someone who is very spiritual or religious. I do accompany my father to the mosque once in a while, especially on Eid. But that is for the inner peace I get out of it. The serenity while offering namaz standing next to my father is unmatched to any experience I have had. I've also been to temples and churches right since I was a kid. This has made me very liberal in my outlook towards religion, and that's how I want my son to be too. Parveen and I have had several discussions on this. As a result, Ayaan knows both Hindu chants and Islamic *dua*s. And he even accompanies my mother in her prayers to Jesus. He greets people with both, 'Salaam Aleikum' and 'Namaste'.

I also learnt that he is much more spiritual than I was at his age. He would pull up a prayer mat every time he saw my father offering namaz and placing it next to him, he would sit on it. He didn't know how to mouth the exact prayers, but he would mimic his grandfather's actions right from the beginning to the final *sajda*, much to the elder's delight. But Ayaan is also a naughty kid. My dad being a little on the orthodox side would get a little flustered when Ayaan would belt out Hindu chants fluently. Noticing this a few times, just to needle him a bit, he would creep up to his grandfather and start saying them out loudly in his ear, much to my dad's annoyance. And then, Ayaan would laugh out loud and switch to the Islamic duas to calm him down. My father too soon caught up with his mischief, so now he just laughs along and tickles him a bit.

I am happy with the way we have brought Ayaan up, instilling in him a respect for all religions and faiths. The first time I did eventually turn to my religion seriously was when I prayed for Ayaan's life. And that's when I realized that there truly is a presence up there who is looking out for you. I would toss and turn in my bed every night since his diagnosis, praying and finding solace in my duas. I learnt that everything, whether you like it or not, happens for a reason.

ELEVEN

CANADA CALLING

'Ayaan, come let me wash your face!'

Parveen towered over Ayaan as he concentrated on the numerous Lego blocks that were strewn all around him. He looked over his shoulder, seemingly annoyed at this unwelcome disruption.

'No,' he said simply. 'My face is fine. I don't want to wash it.'

Parveen shrugged and bent down to lift him up. Ayaan had been particularly fond of Lego, and the love only grew with time, especially in the past few months. He had been advised to rest and not move around much, so Parveen would just hand him his little bucket of Lego blocks and he would spend hours at a stretch making little buildings. He absolutely detested being interrupted during such sessions of serious Lego architecture, so when Parveen asked him to wash his face of all things, he protested a little but then gave in resignedly. With a scowl, he went into the bathroom, wondering why on earth he needed to wash his face. The reason, of course, had nothing to do with the non-existent grime on his skin.

I had flown back from Mumbai on 7 May, and had just arrived in Toronto. Avi had picked me up from the airport and on the way home, we had informed Parveen that I was about to reach. We decided to surprise Ayaan. As we stopped outside the bungalow, I called Parveen again to indicate that I was ready to come in. Once Ayaan had been dragged away to the loo, Parveen's mother opened the door for Avi and me.

I snuck in and tiptoed upstairs towards his room. The blankets on the bed were plush and thick because of the harsh Canadian winters, easy to completely envelope an entire person. I quickly hopped into bed and wrapped myself up with one of the blankets. Ayaan was still in the loo. I was beaming away, relieved and happy to be back. I heard the bathroom door open suddenly and his quick little footsteps shuffled back to where he was earlier seated.

'Ayaan,' I heard Parveen's voice tell him. 'Do you know Nani is very upset with you?'

He was about to sit down and resume playing with his toys, when he heard this latest piece of news. He adored his nani.

'Why, Mama?' he stopped midway and looked at his mother, wide-eyed. 'Nani is upset with me?'

'I don't know, Ayaan! Go ask her,' Parveen replied. 'She is lying down and is waiting to talk to you.'

Ayaan nodded thoughtfully, wondering what he had done to anger his grandmother. He scurried towards the bed, and climbed up. He began to tug at the thick blanket. From underneath, I held it tight. He kept tugging at it with all his might. Finally he succeeded, once I let go. He looked at me dumbstruck.

I had never seen that look on him before. He paused ever so slightly. And then he just leaped and latched on to me, like a panda does to a tree. We all burst out laughing as he locked me in a tight embrace, lying down on top of me!

'Hi Ayaaaaaan,' I began to chuckle, as he buried his head into my chest. I held his head tight against my heart. Once he pulled his head away, he wore a mischievous grin.

'I told you, Mama!' he squealed. 'I knew Papa would come!'

Avi, Parveen and their mother laughed away looking at us. Avi even video-recorded the entire incident on his phone. When he replayed it, it was the most heartbreaking yet heartening video I had ever seen. Here was a four-year-old kid who had accepted the fact that his father had tricked him and left him for a few months to deal with some hospital sessions. He was bitter and angry all the while until he saw his father, right there. He completely let go of all the negative emotions and just hugged me as tight as he could. He was glad to have me back. As for me, there was no place I would rather be. I looked at Ayaan's face. There was a broad smile and I could see his eyes moisten. He looked back and saw the same emotion in my eyes. I still watch that video every now and then. It makes me smile.

The rest of the day proceeded well, with Ayaan spending all his time playing with the new toys and video games that I had brought for him. The two of us sat on the ground, building a Lego house for the latest Batman figurine that I had just brought for him. But every time I looked at him, my heart sank. Ayaan was now a shadow of himself.

His hair was scanty, even though he hadn't lost all of it yet. But his scalp was visible. In fact, even his eyebrows had thinned down. He had lost a lot of weight and was extremely frail. His eyelashes were almost non-existent. Ayaan was more like a wizened old man now than the playful bubbly child I had known all this while. There were plenty of moments when he would just space out and not say or do anything. He might have been introspecting or he could have just been blank. I don't know. But it wasn't usual.

That night was quite an ordeal for me. As Parveen and I lay on either side of Ayaan, we realized that he was tossing and turning more than usual and was extremely queasy. We knew it was the lull before the storm. After his last dose of dactinomycin, the toxicity levels in his body had skyrocketed. After the numerous doses of the chemo drugs—dactinomycin and vincristine—he could almost taste and smell it in his system. I switched on the light and sat up. We noticed that it was close to two in the morning.

'Ayaan,' I whispered. 'Is everything okay?'

He sat up sluggishly and looked at me. He stuck his tongue out in disgust.

'There is some taste in my mouth, Daddy.'

I realized that he was going to throw up. Parveen jumped out of the bed and rushed to the loo to fetch a bucket. As soon as Ayaan saw the bucket, he clambered over to the side of the bed and vomited into it. And that was just the first of many such bouts. He vomited several times during the night, which was pretty alarming.

'This hasn't happened before,' Parveen exclaimed, as Ayaan vomited yet again, almost filling up a second bucket. 'He hadn't vomited this way even once while you were away.'

I was visibly flustered and couldn't bear to see him in such a state any more. Eventually, after filling up three buckets, he stopped. He was exhausted and there was absolutely nothing left in his body. After we washed his face, he hit the bed and fell asleep immediately. Parveen and I, on the other hand, had yet another sleepless night. We figured that this was one of the milder side effects after so many chemotherapy sessions. Ayaan could probably taste the chemo in his mouth which was making him puke.

The next morning, however, Ayaan was his normal self when he woke up. In fact, Parveen told me that he hadn't been this cheerful in a while, and was overjoyed that his father was back. After breakfast, he began tugging at my hand while I was speaking to Avi.

'Come, Daddy,' he said. 'Let's go to the park!'

He clutched a little football under his arm and led me to the park outside. It wasn't snowing much and the weather was pretty good to play around. Some of his new friends were already waiting there for him. They cheered when he arrived and he waved back at them, grinning away.

I watched Ayaan and his buddies play from a seat in the corner of the park. After a while, once they were done, they started walking towards me. I overheard a conversation. One of the kids had asked him about his slight shift in appearance.

'Oh, I had cancer,' Ayaan shrugged. 'Right now the doctors give me chemotherapy. Vincristine and dactinomycin.'

I was stunned when I heard this. I had no clue that Ayaan knew the terminology and the names of the medicines. I have always maintained that he is a sharp child and his ability to grasp information is extraordinary. Children do tend to be like that and register a lot more than we believe they do. Ayaan, in this situation, had probably picked up the words during the several sessions at the hospital. SickKids had told Parveen that we must inform Ayaan that he was fighting cancer and was taking the medicines to recover fully and bounce back. According to them, keeping the child in the dark had adverse psychological effects. Luckily enough for all of us, Ayaan's final chemotherapy session was scheduled on 27 May.

We tried to make it as easy for him as we could. We would take him around to the various parks, to his favourite haunt, Chuck E. Cheese, where he would squeal with delight on spotting the amiable mouse they had as a mascot. His aunt Geena would always take time off from her schedule and come over with goodies for him and take us out to the mall. Even his other aunt, Sherly, would bring her son Rehaan and they would play for hours in the park. We also took him out for several movies including *Godzilla* and the superhero extravaganza—*X-Men: Days of Future Past*. Ayaan had a ball during that film, and as we left the theatre, he looked up at me, debating with himself for a while before he let me in on a secret.

'You know what, Daddy? I am going to be a superhero too,' he said and shifted his gaze.

I smiled back, without wanting to prod any further. He was probably thinking about the Batman conversations. Batman had called him several times while I was away and had spoken to him about how it was important to have those icky veggie smoothies to become Ayaan Man! Batman was extremely helpful throughout the ordeal, as he got Ayaan to obediently do the stuff that his parents couldn't make him do. Right from getting him to eat right to sleep on time to fuss very little over the chemo sessions, Batman was truly the Saviour Knight.

On the morning of his last chemotherapy session, Parveen woke him up at quarter to seven. He brushed his teeth and came back to the room to see Parveen holding out a neatly ironed shirt that he was supposed to wear. He shrieked and ran back into the bathroom. I rushed inside and caught him, before he tried to lock himself in.

'What happened, Ayaan?' I asked him, as he broke into tears.

'I don't want to go there!'

'Where?'

'The hospital,' he sobbed. 'Don't take me to the hospital! Every time Mama takes me there she makes me wear a shirt for chemo!'

When we took him out that morning to the hospital, there was no wild snowstorm. It was now summer in Toronto and the streets were clearer than they had been back in January and February.

Parveen had figured out a way of keeping Ayaan amused in the car. She would buy a new Lego toy for every chemo session and had mastered the art of completing it along with him in that hour-long journey to the hospital. We usually applied a sensation numbing patch over his port in the car, an hour before the chemo session. That morning he protested and how! Avi had to pull the car over, and the two of us had to pin him down and hold his hands as Parveen applied the patch.

After that tussle, Ayaan sat quietly, brimming over with anger. He didn't speak a word. He just ignored us and all our friendly overtures. He even refused the iPad and chose to look outside the window instead. We decided to just let him be and give him some space for a while. Parveen had mentioned to me that Ayaan would exhibit anger quite often. The entire situation had left him frustrated. He didn't like being bogged down this way. He liked his freedom, he liked running around and playing physical sports. The mental and physical exertion was immensely taxing for him, probably even more than it was for us.

As the car pulled up in the dingy car park, Ayaan opened the door and stepped out authoritatively. He walked towards the elevator without waiting for any of us. It was a very 'let's get this done with' kind of air that he wore around him that day. I decided to call him up as Batman to let him know that this was the final dose. The final day.

I made some excuse about parking the car with Avi and let Ayaan and Parveen go up by themselves. And then I punched in her number.

'Someone for you,' Parveen said as she handed Ayaan the phone who answered it brusquely, after getting out of the lift and stepping away from her.

'Yes Batman?' He knew who the 'someone' was right away. No, 'Is that Batman?' this time.

'Ayaan,' I replied. 'Today is the final session of chemo. After this, you will become a superhero.'

I could feel his mood lighten up once he knew that he was attending the final session.

'Are you sure, Batman?'

'Yes,' I replied. 'We are done. No more chemo after today.'

After we finished the call, I went up to see him. He was back to his cheerful self and had run off to the play area. After all this while, Ayaan had become quite popular in the cancer section of the hospital. He has this innate ability of attracting people. He would walk up to everyone and introduce himself, 'Hi, I'm Ayaan Hashmi!' After a couple of hours of waiting, it was finally his turn. All this while, I was just wondering to myself how Parveen had stayed solid as a rock throughout this entire episode. She had single-handedly braved the situation. Despite the emotional turbulence in her, she was the guiding force for Ayaan and the rest of the family. It's no mean feat to be in a foreign country with a child battling for his life and without a husband by her side. I'm certain that if I was in her shoes, I would've cracked under the pressure.

His last session took fifteen minutes. He protested a bit initially, like he usually did when he was made to take the chemo. But it was done in no time. As soon as it was over, Ayaan hopped off the hospital bed and trotted off confidently. Each step that he took exuded bravery, almost as though he had fought a major war and had emerged victorious. This was actually the case, to be honest. He strode out of the room, and I saw for myself how immensely popular he was with the hospital staff, as Parveen had once mentioned to me on the phone. He would wave at and high-five the nurses and call them by their first names. Ayaan was in his element. He shouted out an ecstatic 'bye', like he had conquered and overcome yet another obstacle. At last, the chemo cycle was done! We breathed a sigh of relief.

Of course, the entire procedure hadn't been wrapped up just yet. We needed to extract the port, which was a minor operation that was scheduled ten days after the last chemo. We decided that we would use this break well and take a little holiday. He needed a distraction, and we realized that the Blue Mountain resort in Ontario was the perfect getaway. It was a refreshing change even for Parveen and me, as our moments of solace had been few and far between ever since Ayaan had first urinated blood.

Soon enough, it was time to extract the port. We took Ayaan back to the hospital, and he felt betrayed. After all, Batman had said no more chemo. Nothing about the port removal. I explained the procedure to him as well as I could. I told him that we were going to take out the patch that was strapped up against his chest, and that it was a tiny thing that would take no time at all. However, in reality, it took a good forty-five minutes and Ayaan was sedated with general anaesthesia. After that, he was well and truly done. But with cancer, it's never that simple.

Parveen and I were ecstatic to be going back home. I remember I was packing Ayaan's clothes into his Angry Birds bag when he stormed up to me and looked at me questioningly.

'Where are we going, Papa?'

'Home,' I said, meeting his gaze with a broad smile.

Instead of seeing happiness on his face, I saw surprise.

'I don't want to go back!' he growled. 'I like Canada!'

I was taken aback. Canada had been a nightmarish affair for all of us. And here he stood indignantly, stomping his feet and shouting at me because he didn't want to leave. He was about to pull out all the clothes I had stacked up neatly in his bag. After a few loud protests, I decided to calm him down.

'Okay, okay! Ayaan! I was joking!'

He raised an eyebrow. 'Then where are we going?'

'Bali,' I lied. 'You really enjoyed it there, didn't you? We are off to Bali for another holiday! No hospitals there either!'

He pondered over it for a moment and then shrugged.

'Okay,' he said simply. 'Pack my bag then.'

And then he shuffled away to play with his Lego blocks. I chuckled to myself.

Avi and Gina, Parveen's cousin, had come to drop us off at the airport. Avi was married to a Mexican girl, Paty, who he had separated from. He had two children with her—Sophia and Zara—who lived with Paty in Mexico. He hadn't met them for over four years. He couldn't travel outside Canada due to some issues with his citizenship. For the five months that he was there,

Ayaan filled the void left by Avi's children in his life and made up for their absence. Ayaan too had gotten attached to his uncle and it was a very emotional moment for all of us. Parveen's family had really seen us through this entire ordeal.

'Come back soon, Batman!' Avi and Gina took turns to lift up their nephew. 'Canada will miss you!'

The return journey was via Brussels once again. This time he didn't demand pizzas and burgers. His diet was completely tuned to healthy, organic food with fruit smoothies and wholesome meals. As the plane started it descent over Mumbai on 12 June, Ayaan peeped through the window at a city that was all too familiar. *This isn't Bali,* he thought. As the plane lowered, he realized where we were. *This is Mumbai! Papa tricked me!* He looked at me angrily. He said something, but his voice was drowned under the roaring engine of the plane as the wheels hit the runway. Ayaan began to throw a fit.

'I want to go back to Canada,' I heard him say.

'Calm down,' I said. 'Relax, Ayaan!'

He began to tug at his seat belt and after succeeding to set himself free, he tried to run out. The plane had landed by now and all the other passengers were looking at him amusedly. He was screaming and we had to stop him somehow. We were sitting right ahead, so once the pilot stepped out of the cockpit, he saw us trying to quieten him. The pilot recognized me and Ayaan instantly and asked to have a word with me.

'I read about your son,' he started. 'Was he being treated in Canada?'

'Yes,' I replied. 'He's okay now. He's kicking up a storm because he didn't want to return to Mumbai.'

The pilot smiled and walked up to Ayaan. He held him by the hand and got him to sit down. He bent over and in a low whisper told him something that I couldn't hear, but I saw that it made Parveen smile. Ayaan's protests also came to an abrupt halt. He hopped off the seat and was led by the pilot into the cockpit. The pilot motioned me to join them.

Ayaan gasped once he was inside the cockpit. This was something new for him. He hopped up on the seat and looked at the various buttons, too scared to touch them.

'If I press the buttons and turn the plane around, will we go back to Canada?' He looked up at the pilot.

The pilot and I burst out laughing. I lifted him up into my arms.

'Don't get ideas, Ayaan. We are home now.'

TWELVE

FOR THE CANCER CURIOUS

I have always been very open to taking on experimentative roles as an actor. One such role was of a character incidentally named Ayaan that I played in the Academy Award winning director Danis Tanović's film—*Tigers*. My character was a young, newly married salesman who gets a job to peddle locally made drugs to pharmacies and doctors. Despite the fact that the Pakistani-manufactured pharmaceuticals he sells are much cheaper than those sold by Western competitors, no one trusts or buys his products as they lack major brand names. He then goes on to join a renowned multinational company. When Ayaan discovers the company's baby formula has killed hundreds of children, he begins a lone and dangerous battle against the company. The film is set in reality, and traces the entire journey of the character who challenges the system in what is reminiscent of a David vs Goliath battle.

At the time of writing this book, the film is yet to be released in India theatrically, but it has gathered acclaim in the international film circuit. I had finished filming it long ago, but thinking about it recently made me draw several parallels to reality. For one, how we are misled by profit-hungry multinationals and coaxed into believing that some things are good for us. How something as simple and harmless as sugar can wreak havoc in our systems.

Sugar? The stuff that makes cheesecakes taste that good? The stuff that makes cookies so satiating? Oh well, probably it's bad for the teeth. Yep, heard that one. Or too much of it can lead to diabetes. Yeah, well, I'll brush my teeth and won't have too much of it. I'll be careful, now go bring me my cola.

THE BITTERSWEET REALITY

You may have heard of the consequences in passing and probably scoffed them off. I was just like that too. But there are certain bitter truths about sugar that I came across while studying cancer extensively, that made me change my diet. In fact, after what happened to Ayaan, we were all so shaken up that we decided to undergo a radical change with our lifestyles. I want to bring to your notice some of my findings. There is one bit of information that should shake you up and make you cut down on your sugar intake drastically. Here it goes . . . *Sugar feeds cancer!* Now some may argue that sugar feeds every cell in our body and the cancer cell is no different. While that is true, the difference is that it essentially encourages tumour growth.

The sugar intake in our diet is responsible not just for the obesity epidemic but for heart disease, type-2 diabetes and the soaring rates of cancer. The problem lies not just in the excess consumption of calories through sugar but in the way our bodies metabolize sugar. Let me draw your attention to the case of high fructose corn syrup, which is a fruit sugar that makes up 50 per cent of the refined sugar we consume. There is no hormone in our system to remove fructose from our bloodstream, unlike glucose, which stimulates insulin, a hormone that allows the body to use sugar. It is then left to the liver to remove it and when the liver is overwhelmed it converts fructose to liver fat, which ups our chances of developing insulin resistance (a precursor to diabetes), hardened arteries and heart disease. Secondly, fructose suppresses the hormone leptin, which indicates when we are full, as a result of which our brain lets us consume it without limit. The amount of fructose lurking in your average juice carton also depends on whether the manufacturer has added extra sugar. However, to give you an idea of why anti-sugar campaigners are so worried about fruit juice is because a cup and a half of unsweetened apple juice contains nine teaspoons of sugar, which is more than what a can of cola contains!

Every tumour has insulin receptors, which makes the cancer cells absorb the sugar ten to twelve times more than the normal rate of healthy cells. The consequence of ingesting a lot of sugar is that your blood sugar levels will quickly rise to a point that is detrimental to your general health. It also causes a spike in insulin. Firstly, sugar by itself is a great stimulant and fuels hungry cancer cells. Secondly, the excess insulin produced acts as a stimulating factor that supports cell growth, cell division, and ultimately multiplication of these bad cells. It is important that you keep a watch on your carbohydrate intake as excessive eating increases the blood sugar level.

To radically cut our sugar intake would be to radically shake up the economy. According to Zoë Harcombe, nutritionist and author of *The Obesity Epidemic*:

> The commercial food producers, who rely on sugar, represent a huge and powerful lobby. It's not just the obvious brands, such as fizzy drinks manufacturers, that would suffer if sugar were removed from our diets. Sugar is added to just about everything you buy ready-made: bread, sauces, ready meals, drinks, tinned foods . . . The list is endless.

I read about this experiment where a doctor conducted a positron emission tomography (a PET scan), which is an imaging test that checks for diseases in the body with radioactive tracers in a special dye. The doctor made the patient drink sugared water and noted that it gets taken preferentially to the cancer cells, which light up brightly because they consume more sugar in comparison to the healthy cells! Furthermore, Otto Warburg, the 1931 Nobel Laureate in Medicine, discovered that malignant tumours exhibit increased glycolysis, which means that the cancer is fuelled by glucose. Sugar also drops immunity by hampering the process of phagocytosis, which, to put it simply, is the process of engulfing of impurities for the purpose of building immunity. And then of course, the most obvious problem that sugar brings to the table is obesity.

One interesting fact is that, progressively, consumers are buying fewer bags of sugar, that is, 'visible sugar'. However, there is a phenomenal increase in 'invisible sugar', the sort the food industry sneaks into their products.

I find it really confusing that some of the biggest cancer centres in the world actually advise their patients to eat sugar-heavy products. I remember while Ayaan was being treated and was drastically losing weight he was asked to have a baby meal replacement that had an alarmingly high sugar content. They recommend this so that he would regain his regular weight. But apart from sugar, many food products also have another harmful ingredient called Monosodium Glutamate (MSG). Another hidden name for it is Hydrolysed Vegetable Protein. You will see it on the packets of chips. It is known as the Umami taste and is very addictive.

Some doctors, oncologists included, hand over a candy from a bowl on their desk to kids after every visit to cheer them up! I mean, if doctors are doing this, who's going to question and elucidate the problems sugar brings up? But all you have to do is read a little and educate yourselves. After reading up, I have made radical changes to not just Ayaan's diet, but even mine and Parveen's. In fact, I tell everyone I can to cut their sugar intake and look out for alternatives to sugar. And when I say alternatives, I don't mean switch to diet soda instead of the usual soda pop (which incidentally has twelve teaspoons of sugar for every can). Artificial sweeteners (aspartame, saccharin, etc.) are as bad, if not worse than the real sugar! They can cause several problems like heart palpitations, migraines, depression and nausea. The list is endless. So steer clear of them. Instead, turn to natural replacements like honey, maple syrup, or organic jaggery. Brown sugar is not exactly good either because the stuff we get here is either coloured or caramelized white sugar. A good substitute to sugar is Xylitol, a birch-bark extract, which is highly sweetening but contains only one-third of the calories of other sugars. It does not cause blood sugar or insulin levels to spike either. It is also the only sugar that has been linked to a decrease in the risk of dental cavities. So that's a great substitute, though it not widely available in India and is slightly expensive. Whenever I have a cup of tea, I drop in a bit of honey instead of that cute little sugar cube.

In fact, I had visited Ayaan's school once, after his treatment. When I spoke to his teacher, she had a funny anecdote to share. The principal had walked into their class one day and decided to ask a few questions. Whoever would get them right would get a packet of candies or mints. When Ayaan heard of this, he apparently stood up and protested wildly.

'Mint has sugar!' he shrieked. 'And sugar feeds cancer. Don't give little children that!'

The principal, needless to say, was taken aback! When I heard it, I too was shocked. But then I broke into a proud smile. I have taught my son well!

THE BURZYNSKI BROUHAHA

Even though I opted for conventional cancer therapy for my son's treatment, I want to put a few more options out there. This is partly because I learnt about all of this only once Ayaan's treatment was under way. I read an interesting analogy in a book called *Knockout* by Suzanne Somers and began to think of chemotherapy this way—your body is a nation and a part of it has been invaded by the bad guys. Now to get them out, you send out your army, air force, military and completely carpet-bomb the area until it's devoid of the villains. Now that certainly does get the job done, but the collateral damage it causes is fairly serious and in some cases even insurmountable. It is completely logical to get the cancer cells out of the body. But what if you stopped the cancer cells from dividing instead? Wouldn't the cancer disappear? This is a pertinent question that will crop up in everyone's mind once they read about Dr Stanislaw Burzynski and his understanding and ways of treatment.

As was the case with my character in *Tigers*, where I took on a large, greedy system, Dr Burzynski and several others who found alternatives to chemotherapy also realized how difficult it is to take on the men with the money, power, clout and control. Cancer is where the money lies. It's a business. And finding a cure could probably mean losing out on billions of dollars. In a nutshell, I will describe to you Dr Burzynski's case, and then it's up to you to make what you may of it. I am not going to try to influence your opinion, just subtly inform you of what I've come across.

To understand his research, you must know what a peptide is. It's a molecule consisting of two or more amino acids. These are smaller than proteins, which are chains of fifty or more amino acids. Anything under that is generically referred to as peptides. According to Dr Stanislaw Burzynski's research, certain peptides called antineoplastons are missing in cancer patients. These are produced by the liver and control cell multiplication, thereby working as an internal controlling agent. Dr Burzynski deduced that in the absence of these internal containing agents, the cancer cells go out of control and fester into a tumour. Burzynski's treatment, which he meted out in his clinic, involved replacing these missing peptides to knock out the cancer. He was pretty successful too and in an interview he even claims that on some occasions entire tumours have vanished! But the clinic has been the focus of criticism and had several legal cases slapped on it and his medication was not approved by the Food and Drug Administration. Now I am not an advocate of Dr Burzynski, because I have certainly not had my son treated at his clinic. But I suggest you read up about him, if you are interested to check out this one unconventional possibility.

THE LAETRILE COVER-UP

A similar case that I had read about and that had kicked up quite a storm was regarding the compound laetrile, which prevented the spread of cancer. Laetrile was a patented drug made from the natural compound amygdalin, which is found in the seeds of fruits like apricots, apples, plums and even in almonds. Amygdalin contains glucose, benzaldehyde and cyanide. And it was this cyanide that had the anti-cancer properties. But the catch was that cyanide was also toxic to all cells, in general. But in the doses laetrile was administered, it wasn't exactly detrimental. And the chances of getting poisoned by apple or apricot seeds and dying are next to none. The drug underwent trial tests by a certain Japanese doctor and was found to be extremely effective. One of the world's largest research centres in the 1970s had initially even signed off on the clinical trials. But then suddenly, they took a U-turn and refuted the Japanese doctor's claims and said that laetrile wasn't effective. This despite laetrile showing concrete results, even after their verdict. It was a clear case of a cover-up. The guys who ran the centre were influential and some of the board members were directors, chairmen, presidents of manufacturers of chemotherapy drugs. Was there a conflict of interest? Clearly, as they realized that laetrile was not profitable as an alternative treatment. Apricot seeds cost next to nothing. The drugs for chemotherapy, on the other hand, are extremely expensive and burn a hole in your pocket while it fills up someone else's. Once again, from what I can gather from my readings, there is some sort of injustice here. And in a bid to make money and quench their greed, corporates are putting people's lives at stake since there are patients who are being denied access to potential treatments. I have read so much about this, that somewhere down the line, I can't help but wonder if the medical system in the world has been calculatedly created to make money instead of curing people.

THE UNLIKELY DRUG

Even hemp oil has been restricted as an alternative treatment method, despite not presenting any real danger. Many large pharmaceutical companies that still run shop today, used to sell hemp-based medications back in the 1900s. If taken orally, the cannaboids the oil contain had properties that sought out cancerous cells and destroyed them effectively. In fact, I read that hemp oil had many medicinal values apart from its cancer-killing properties. If, for example, you apply it topically on a severe burn or ulcer repeatedly for three days, the affected area will be cured completely! It was even found to be extremely useful in the treatment of skin cancer. But then again, once greed crept in, all the governments chose to do was rename hemp as marijuana and harp upon how it was a drug that was detrimental to health. I read about this in a book by Rick Simpson titled *Nature's Answer for Cancer,* and was quite surprised to realize that something as basic as hemp oil had such properties! But then again, how would anyone really know, if doctors prescribe chemotherapy to you without even considering to let you know about the natural options that exist?

CAUSES OF CANCER AND THE CHEMO CONFLICT

Chemotherapy by itself is flawed, as I have come to understand. As of now, it's more like a standard 'one size fits all' approach. The truth is that each case of cancer is different and has to be tackled accordingly. Let me borrow an analogy from the game of cricket—you don't play a hook shot to a full-length ball, do you? Similarly, most patients in India aren't even made aware of the concept of a chemosensitivity test. These are tests which determine whether the chemo that a patient is going to be administered is a fit or not. The cancer cells are harvested out of an affected person's blood, then broken down genetically and from there after about a week or two one can determine which drug is ideal for the treatment. Had I known about such a procedure when Ayaan was initially diagnosed with cancer, I would've definitely considered it.

It is really crucial to understand what causes cancer. The cancer cell stems from a very short strand of DNA within the helix. Every human being contains this specific strand of DNA which is triggered off if there is a lack of oxygen. Once the body reaches a particular low oxygen environment, this particular gene begins to form cancer cells. From what I have gathered thus far, there are a few reasons which lead to cancer. To start with, if you have a weak immune system, you are certainly more susceptible to the illness. Improper nutrition, stress, emotional shocks, ageing and several reasons prove to be catalysts that weaken your immunity.

Secondly, an unhealthy diet definitely increases your chances of cancer. Cancer thrives in acidic environments—acidic foods like soda, coffee, processed foods and fast foods, deep-fried foods, red meats, artificial sweeteners, are all agents that contribute to cancer if consumed regularly. The transfats, unhealthy oils and other chemicals in such foods suffocate the cells and deprive the body of oxygen. And if there's no oxygen in the body, the cancer cells begin to thrive. I, for one, have cut these out to a large extent.

I have greatly reduced sugar, meat, dairy and refined foods. I have increased my vegetable and fruit intake. I try and pick up a lot of organic foods, especially when I'm abroad, and I drink only filtered water at all times to avoid unwanted fluoride and chlorine. I also add a pinch of turmeric to all the food I consume and I suggest you do too, because it has proven cancer-inhibiting properties. I have cut down considerably on my red meat consumption, because it is high in absorbable iron which is a major carcinogen. Even if you do enjoy your red meat, accompany it with a generous serving of veggies. The natural folic acid found in leafy green vegetables like broccoli, sprouts and cauliflower boost the body's defence mechanism against cancer. In fact, Ayaan is extremely fond of broccoli, which he laps up readily as an evening snack! I even prepare a shake which contains two-thirds of a cup of paneer, six tablespoons of flaxseed oil and a lot of berries and nuts (not peanuts). This is known as the Budwig shake, named after a German biochemist. This unlikely shake works wonders in increasing the oxygen level in the cells and produces energy in the body. Initially, Ayaan was a little squeamish about it, but once Parveen and I began having it to show him it's not bad, he joined us happily!

We live in a hazardous environment. There are dangerous toxins in household products like air fresheners, cleaning products, etc. Even bodycare products, aerosols, etc. have a lot of these harmful chemicals. If you are a smoker, I don't even have to elaborate and warn you of the consequences as the packet of cigarettes tells you all you need to know. Besides, the pollution in the environment is so high that it causes a lot of other diseases, not just cancer. And adding to that, we have our Wi-Fi units and cellular networks turned on at all times, which is nothing but waves passing through our bodies and disrupting the balance from the inside slowly and steadily. These are all things that can't really be eradicated from our lives, unless you want to live like a sage.

But we must keep all of this in mind at all times. I always switch off the Wi-Fi units and keep my phone away from my bed before sleeping. I have learnt to make these small changes in my lifestyle because there is no more room for error after going through what we did with Ayaan!

Cancer is a disease of the whole body whereas the tumour is just a symptom. We all have cancer cells in our body, but it takes a billion such cells to come together to form a lump. And as I had mentioned earlier on, surgery can spread cancer and lead to metastasis. The very rationale of surgery is to take out the cancer and try to kill it. But that isn't the end of it. We have to take the right measures and be extremely cautious. The choice of treatment, whether conventional or not, is entirely personal. Obviously, after having written all of this down, I myself would've been in two minds had I known the alternatives to chemotherapy as soon as Ayaan was diagnosed. I would not have been very comfortable going against the trained doctors' suggestions and trying out something unconventional. Medical ignorance can be dangerous and I wanted you to have a rough idea of the things that I feel are important for you to know. I do not shun conventional treatment in any way as the standard treatment protocol worked for Ayaan, but I want you to take a second opinion, or as many opinions as it takes, to educate yourself.

The fact is that cancer isn't just a disease that ravages your body. It even tears you apart mentally. Based on my experience and research, I have compiled a few tips which I'll state at the end of the book, where it is the easiest to refer to them.

THIRTEEN

AYAAN RETURNS

We were back to our normal routine once we returned to Mumbai after Ayaan's treatment in Canada. The dust had settled, so to speak. When Parveen first went to drop him to school, Little Bo Peep in Khar, he seemed thrilled throughout the car ride. Once he stepped out and walked through the gates of his school, after all this while, he squealed excitedly and rushed towards his friends. He embraced them tightly and all of them rejoiced loudly, yelling, 'Welcome back, Ayaan!' There was a lump in my throat when Parveen recounted that to me, so I can only imagine how she would have felt when she witnessed it. Our son had missed out on a few precious months of school, the fun days he would never get back! Nevertheless, he was completely ecstatic to be reunited with his little friends and that was heartening. There was this one instance back in Canada when he realized that he was going to miss out on a dance competition held at the St Andrew's Auditorium in Bandra. He had really been looking forward to participate in it, but alas, it wasn't meant to be. At least for that year. Throughout all of this, we were informed that his friends would enquire about him on a daily basis. In fact, we learnt that in his absence, all of Ayaan's classmates and teachers would start their day with a little prayer for him!

In the meantime, we were trying to forget the entire phase of Ayaan's treatment in Canada and get on with our lives. In the months that followed, Ayaan seemed mostly unaffected by the treatment and was still the spunky kid he used to be. He did start getting nightmares though and would sometimes shout in his sleep. And just when we would think he's improving substantially, a demon of a memory would pop out from somewhere and cause him to react. For instance, one morning, to get him dressed for school, Parveen had ironed a cute powder-blue shirt and laid it out for him. As soon as he stepped out of the bathroom and saw the shirt, an alarm went off in his head. *It's early morning and Mama has kept a shirt for me to wear . . . Mama and Papa are taking me for chemo!*

'NO!' he bellowed. 'I am not going to the hospital!'

Parveen and I looked at him confusedly.

'You are making me wear a shirt!' he protested. 'That means you are taking me for chemo!'

It was then that we understood what he meant. The shirt was a mental trigger. As I had mentioned earlier, a shirt made the port that was installed in his chest more accessible than a T-shirt did, when the chemo had to be administered. And now, even after a few months since we had returned from Toronto, just looking at a shirt at seven in the morning brought back all the bad memories!

Despite these stray incidents we were relieved that he continued to be cheerful, and was getting back into the groove slowly and steadily.

When Ayaan was first diagnosed, I felt a sense of helplessness and powerlessness. It was like I had hit a wall. There was an overbearing feeling of guilt. *Where had I gone wrong? Did I mess up as a parent?* I spoke to several doctors and oncologists, and the advice they gave me was very useful and I am thankful to them. There were many unanswered questions, too, and they were taken aback by the research I had done! The reason they gave for the cause of cancers, is mostly, genetic. But if you go by Charles Darwin, the father of genetics theory, and his concept about the survival of the fittest, it says that if there was a gene coded for cancer there would be less of the disease, because people with that gene would be deselected from the herd. But quite contrary to this belief, we are seeing more of it. In the next decade or so, cancer rates will go up from two in four people to three in four people. That is why there is a new field of research called 'epi-genetics' which states that there is a big difference between a gene and a mutated gene, but nobody questions what caused the gene to mutate in the first place. You would think that they do, but they don't. Also, there is no holistic methodology which attempts to discover the causative nature of cancer and what we need to do to fix it. In Ayaan's case of the Wilms' tumour, that was what every doctor told me, right from Mumbai to Toronto.

I also felt that I wasn't contributing enough to the well-being and recovery of my son. I didn't want to fail as a parent. My contribution was only financial, and that wasn't enough. It made me angry. Adding to that anger and tension was the doctors' responses when I asked them if Ayaan would be cancer-free after his chemo ended: 'Hopefully, he will.' There was a question mark that lingered at the end of every conversation and there was never a sense of finality or conclusiveness. At no point did I get to hear from any doctor, 'Yes, he will recover fully.' Parents are psychologically at ease when they see their children on their way to recovery and that the drugs are doing the job. But once the treatment ended, and the chemo stopped, we worried that the drug wasn't in the body bombarding the bad cells any more. The entire scenario sent our mental well-being for a toss!

The truth is, when someone is diagnosed with a disease like cancer, it's not just the patient who suffers immensely. The people around them are constantly distressed too. Especially the person (or a set of persons) who has to undertake the role of caregiver, usually in the immediate family, is the most crucial contact in a cancer patient's life. There are common elements of sadness and depression that pervades everyone's minds. While the diagnosis can be the most horrifying moment in a person's life and can send their life down in a spiralling tizzy, it is important for the immediate family to overcome the shock and the perpetual feeling of sadness that will accompany it. I know that overcoming it is easier said than done, but you cannot let it show, especially in front of the patient. In Ayaan's case, he never really knew the gravity of the situation. 'Cancer', even when he learnt the word, was probably just name of a disease. He might have known it was more serious than a common cold, but I don't think he knew the terminal nature of the illness. He must have also figured that Mama and Papa weren't making him go through the rigorous medical regimes at hospitals because they wanted him to suffer.

When Parveen and I had first heard of his diagnosis, she was in a constant state of denial. As was I for a certain extent of time. Our family and friends were an immense support, but I grieved alone. I didn't show my emotions and covered up my pain with external bravado, but there were times when I felt weak. After Ayaan was diagnosed, I started praying at night which I never used to before. But we had to overcome and accept the fact that he had cancer because we needed to move forward and get our son treated instead of mulling over the situation. The pain you see your loved ones go through can harm you adversely too. The role you are playing as a caregiver is extremely taxing, especially if the patient in question is a kid. Parveen and I both had trouble sleeping and a general sense of fatigue, right from the day he was diagnosed, engulfed us. The depression I went through manifested itself in the form of many symptoms, like the stress-related pain in my left arm, palpitations, loss of appetite and sleep-related disorders. In fact, thinking about that entire ordeal still shakes me up. But it is imperative to stay positive, because only then can one guide the patient through their steps of recovery. We could never let our guard down and show Ayaan our feelings when we interacted with him. Instead, we had to put on our smiling faces and engage him in activities that he found interesting and amusing. Similarly, if you are dealing with a patient who is entirely aware of what cancer is and can do, you should help them out with housework and personal care as the disease, and subsequent treatment would have made them fragile and weak. Adding to that are the side effects (appetite loss, nausea, fever, acute physical pain, etc.) which saps the energy from their body completely. You must also ensure that the patient gets sufficient undisturbed sleep. This is a very important step to the road of recovery as that is the time when the cells repair themselves. Keeping the affected person engaged in activities that they enjoy is also necessary because you can't let the patient feel like they are handicapped in any way.

Ayaan would often question his scanty hair and shrivelled looks. Batman would call him up and tell him that it was all a part of the process of becoming Ayaan Man. But you can't convince someone older with such stories. The loss of self-esteem is a dangerous side effect that can lead the patient to lose their confidence and question their own abilities. Ayaan would exhibit a lot of anger. He would grit his teeth and not talk to us for long periods of time. At first, I thought that it was because of his childishness, but I realized that it's very common amongst people who have been diagnosed and undergone cancer treatments. He would sit for long gaps in time where he would completely space out and only respond cursorily. It wasn't the Ayaan I knew. I could no longer guess what was going on in his mind.

You have to tell the patient not to lose heart and do your best to keep their confidence intact, and never let them fall prey to a negative state of mind. You have to tell them that their anxiety and fear is without good reason and that everything will be okay. Staying optimistic is their greatest strength and fortunately, just like a malignant tumour, even optimism does multiply. It is very important to realize that cancer does not equal to death. The two aren't synonymous. It's a lot about the attitude that a patient and their support system have.

I feel in India we need a more comprehensive service offered to patients diagnosed with cancer and their families. Psychosocial oncology is the need of the hour. The word 'psychosocial' may seem intimidating, but it helps to break down what it means. 'Psycho', in this context, relates to the mind, or psyche, and the 'social' is about the relationships people have with family and society. Oncology, of course, is the branch of medicine that deals with cancer. Psychosocial oncology, therefore, is a speciality in cancer care concerned with understanding and treating psychological, emotional, social, spiritual and even financial aspects, from prevention through bereavement. It is a personal approach to cancer care that addresses a range of human needs that can improve the quality of life for people affected by cancer. And by this I don't mean traditional psychologists. It has to be cancer specific. People should understand that caregivers, friends and family members of patients, also require emotional support and counselling as a cancer cases in the family can have an emotional and psychological impact on every individual who is supporting a diagnosed patient. In fact, Parveen and I still feel we need to visit or consult a psychiatrist now and then, even after Ayaan has been treated successfully, to assure us that he will be okay.

I remember Smiley, my cousin, consulting her astrologist during Ayaan's nephrectomy in Hinduja Hospital. She had asked him if his kidney would be saved in the operation and he had promptly replied that it would. But that hadn't been the case. I remember scoffing at the thought of consulting astrologers, but I was so desperate for people to tell me that Ayaan would be all right that even I resorted to that! I consulted several astrologers and fortune-tellers as crazy as it may sound. I had literally tried every possible thing that could bring me comfort. Everything that would reinforce my belief in the fact that nothing would happen to my son. The film fraternity is big on astrology and fortune-telling, and I was taken by a friend to a tarot card reader in Juhu. It was an eerie experience. The woman knew stuff that nobody else, save me, did—things that happened when I was in school and college and weren't known to the media or were in the public domain. As spooky as it was, I realized one thing. These people usually got the past spot-on, but with the future, it was always a hit or miss. At the end of it all, however, most of them told me the one thing that I did want to hear. *Ayaan is going to be fine . . .* I went to quite a few astrologers just to get my constant fix of reassurance. Of course, I heard some ridiculous theories too, that Ayaan was probably paying off a karmic debt for something evil that he had done in his past life, or something like that. I cancelled that bit out and only stuck to the part that I needed to hear. And I knew I wasn't going to stop with this new irrational hobby. Once I landed in Canada, I met some soothsayers there too, and even spoke to one over the phone! I wanted everyone to be on the same page with respect to the possibilities of Ayaan making it out alive, be it doctors or astrologers. I tried every possible thing that could bring me the solace I needed. Everything that would reinforce my belief in the fact that nothing would happen to my son. But now that I think of it, I would've been in a much better place had I consulted a psychosocial oncologist.

Research validates that emotional and psychosocial distress is often experienced in the form of depression and other difficulties, and is a significant problem for at least half of all cancer patients. There is the need for a large variety of counselling and support programmes to be made available through hospitals and medical institutes in India, including those designed to help people cope with cancer from the initial stage of diagnosis, through

their treatments, to adjusting to post-treatment side effects.
Psychosocial counselling can help alleviate emotional suffering
and assist in confronting the many issues that arise during the
difficult times. Without this support, patients often struggle and
feel isolated while coping with significant issues such as feeling
vulnerable about their fate and dealing with complex questions
around the quality of their lives. The compounding of these issues
along with the physical pain (in patients) and the manifestations
of stress (in caregivers) can completely destroy your state of living
and well-being.

It is also necessary in the post-treatment stage, where the
side effects come into play. Ayaan had lost most of his hair
and his appearance had changed completely. This had shaken
us up as parents. We needed to be assured that he would
not end up looking like this for the rest of his life. And the
trauma and emotional scars in his mind were a separate issue
altogether. I don't know the exact extent to which the treatment
left a psychological impact, because after the treatment his
demeanour had changed for the first few months. He would
still find joy in his toys and superhero-related stuff, but it was
a lot different initially. Before he was diagnosed with cancer,
Ayaan had this extremely adorable habit of laughing in his sleep.
But this changed after we returned from Canada. However, the
scars were evident, especially in his sleep, when he would yell
in fear, scream for help and shout out a bunch of 'Nos'. Maybe
the 'Nos' were because he was dreaming of the needles that he
had been poked with regularly. It would leave Parveen and me
distressed in the middle of the night.

The fear of recurrence is a different ball game altogether. You
may have fought the cancer, but you can never forget it, as it is
always at the back of your mind. You don't consciously think
about it, but you carry it everywhere you go. You kind of learn to
live with it, you learn to put it on the back burner, but suddenly,

it surfaces again, at times when you least expect it to. Living with uncertainty is never easy. Parveen and I always have the dark cloud looming over us. Every time we think Ayaan is feeling low or if he complains of an ordinary ache or pain, we think that it is the sign of the cancer recurring. Even though we've been assured by the doctor that it's highly unlikely, the fear of the cancer returning is one that stresses me out the most. This is the reason why I made it a point to be well informed, to have regular follow-ups with the doctor and adopt healthy lifestyle choices to build his immunity. As of now, Ayaan has been cancer-free for more than two years. He is very resilient, just like every kid who has battled cancer and lost a chunk of their childhood for no fault of theirs.

The patients, especially kids, are, however, at the risk of developing long-term side effects, also called late-effects, caused by the cancer treatment. Late-effects can be physical or emotional. Not all survivors develop these long-term side effects; it depends on the type of treatment a child had and the age at which they got treated. Emotional difficulties, second cancers, reproductive problems, growth and hormone problems, learning and memory problems, dental problems, vision problems, breathing problems, and heart problems are all late-effects that can hit the patient. Thinking about it makes me queasy, but as of now, even the doctor says that the chances of Ayaan suffering from these are low, even though they are a possibility.

Ayaan is back to normal now, more or less. The 'normal' that I refer to is not the 'normal' it used to be. It's all very different. We are extremely cautious with every action we take. I think everyone who has had a family member who has dealt with this disease can relate to what I am talking about. But it's getting better now. He is healthy again. His hair is back and it's thicker than ever. He eats his broccoli without any fuss. In fact, he savours it and it's his favourite evening snack. He is back to being his chirpy self, which is extremely heartening for us as parents. He is keen on dancing after having watched a few Hindi films. So Parveen has enrolled him in dance classes, which double up as good exercise. He is as bubbly as he used to be. And more importantly, he has begun laughing in his sleep once again.

FOURTEEN

THE LITTLE KNIGHT RISES

A year since Ayaan was discharged from SickKids, things were inching back to normalcy. Ayaan was in good health, regaining all the weight he had lost, his hair had grown back and he was as energetic as ever. Our family had almost recovered from the entire episode. Conversations about cancer and chemo were a thing of the past. That's when life threw another huge obstacle in our paths.

It was cancer again; it had decided to visit our home once more—this time it was my mom. She was diagnosed with hepatocellular carcinoma, cancer of the liver. She had a condition called non-alcoholic fatty liver disease (NAFLD) ever since she was twenty-five years old. It is a term used to describe the accumulation of fat in the liver of people who drink little or no alcohol. NAFLD is quite common, often without any signs or symptoms, and for most people it does not cause any complications. But in some people the fat that accumulates can cause inflammation and scarring in the liver. In my mother's case, the inflammation led to a more serious abnormality—cancer!

Thanks to everything I had read about cancer the reasons came up pretty clear to me: she didn't have the best diet (it was very high on fructose corn syrup), had very erratic sleeping habits and didn't get any exercise. To top that, she was constantly popping harsh painkillers to get relief post her dental surgeries. All of these are key causes to whip up an inflammation in an already sluggish organ.

We put her onto the prescribed medical protocol at Tata Memorial Hospital. The first session was of radioembolization which didn't really help in shrinking the tumour the way we expected. The second session had her take chemotherapy to which the tumour reacted pretty well. Its activity went down considerably. We were thrilled with the results. Obviously, we thought with a couple of more chemo sessions she would pull through, stopping the cancer in its tracks.

I flew off to Bucharest for a film shoot. It was the same day as she was discharged from the hospital after taking a second session of chemotherapy. I remember hugging her and telling her, 'You will be fine. Just eat well and please walk, your body is meant to move. You will be amazed at how fast you will heal if you just stick to a disciplined lifestyle of good food and exercise. If nature has given you a problem, nature can fix it, your own immune system can fix it. Just help your body heal.' I spoke to her a couple of times on the phone from Bucharest and was very stern with her because she was being extremely stubborn. She wouldn't eat, only surviving on juices, and barely moved out of her room.

She finally listened to me two days before my shoot wrapped up. She understood that she had to get better not just for herself but for us, especially for her grandson Ayaan who adored her. She had to live for him. She liked reading storybooks to him while he asked her hundreds of questions. She loved that, it made her feel alive . . . she had to do it for him.

My shoot finally ended, and I was on my way to the airport to catch a flight back home when my dad called. He could barely talk. I could almost hear him hold back his tears, 'Emi, Mummy's in a very bad condition, she fainted and her BP has fallen drastically. I don't know what happened. She's in the ICU.' I couldn't believe what I was hearing. 'Dad, nothing will happen. She will be fine.

It must be because she's very weak. She hasn't been eating, she will be fine.' By the time I got to the airport things got progressively worse. Apparently my dad didn't know but her heart had stopped beating even as she was being wheeled into the hospital. They were trying to revive her.

I was boarding the flight when I made one last call to get an update on her status. My dad picked up, and when he didn't say anything my heart knew what was coming. He finally spoke up, 'She's gone, Emi, she's gone. Come back.' These words echoed in my ears throughout the flight. None of it made sense. I later found out that the reason for her death was a massive cardiac arrest.

After my return, I wanted to get to the bottom of things and know the reason for her stroke. So I called up numerous doctors. The oncologists said that hers was a freak case and that the cancer or the chemotherapy had nothing to do with the stroke. But other doctors told us that chemotherapy always plays havoc with the body, and at her age and with her type of cancer, we shouldn't have given her the chemo. After hearing all these opinions, when I sat down and typed out this final bit for my book, to give the readers my takeaway from all of this, the big question that I had to ask myself was: if I could turn back time would I do things differently, would I put her on chemo?

To find a definite answer unfortunately isn't that easy, the chemo may or may not have been the cause of the heart attack. If we hadn't given her the chemo, she might have survived a few more months or years. But as her family we would not have been able to forgive ourselves if the cancer had spread to other parts of her body. We would have had to always live with the guilt that we did not do enough, we did not put her onto the prescribed medical protocol. I'm sure all these questions will keep haunting me for the rest of my life. But having said that, my family, and millions of families around the world, do what they feel is best for their loved ones and hope for the best results.

Eventually, it all comes down to collateral damage caused by the chemo, especially in patients over the age of sixty. Is it worth putting them through all this suffering when we know the outcome will be so poor? I still feel that if she had followed a healthy lifestyle, with exercise, and supplemented her diet with vitamins and minerals, her body would have equipped itself to slow the cancer with its own defences. Oncologists would obviously snigger at this statement, but my experiences have reinforced my belief in nature.

~

Three months after his recovery, Parveen had a huge argument with Ayaan one evening, before his school's Annual Sports Day. He had come back home from school earlier that day, and was very angry because of the tiff he had had with Parveen in the car on the way back. He flung his bag down and went straight into his room, without even acknowledging me as I opened the front door for them.

'What happened?' I asked Parveen. She looked exhausted.

'They have their Sports Day tomorrow,' she replied. 'He wants to run. The field is huge and they have a race.'

I understood the problem right away. Parveen probably told him not to run. I would've done the same. He was still weak and would get tired very easily. But of course, when Parveen said that, it caused him to get angry. I walked into his room and caught him sulking.

'Papa, I want to run tomorrow.'

His tone was flat and adamant.

'I want to run and I want to win.'

I scratched my chin and looked at him. It was going to be really sunny and I didn't want him to be exposed to that kind of heat. The exertion was inevitable, and he couldn't afford to waste his energy just yet. Not while he was recovering. Plus, the dust.

I didn't want him inhaling the dry, dusty air on some muddy playground. But he had made up his mind. He wanted to run and he wanted to win. *What does one say to that?*

'Okay,' I said, lifting him up in my arms. 'You can run tomorrow. Now give Papa a hug!'

The next morning, I remember sitting in the front row with Parveen, as the Sports Day kicked off with huge fanfare. Parveen and I were both immensely worried as the time for his race drew closer. We were nervous and kept making conversation with each other to distract ourselves. Ayaan was sitting in a separate stand with all the other participants. My eyes were fixed on him, watching him wait eagerly to get on the track and start racing. He was smiling and clapping away, chatting with his friends. I wanted to see him run, but hoped that he wouldn't get disappointed if he didn't win. I was already preparing a speech for him in my head that would tell him that it was okay to lose and that he would win the next time. And that I was going to buy him gifts because I was happy that he had at least participated. My heart felt proud about the fact that he wanted to run, but my mind was worried because I felt that he might just not be able to complete the race.

Soon, it was time. The kids were assembled and made to stand in order behind a white line. He turned around and spotted Parveen and I waving at him. He waved back and then turned around, taking the stance of a well-trained runner. And then, it was time for the race to begin. *On your marks . . . Get set . . . GO!*

As soon as the shrill whistle went off, the other boys started running furiously. It wasn't a professional race, but a fun one where the kids had to do a few cute tasks along the way, before crossing over the finish line. Ayaan started off slowly and began to run. He took exactly three steps and stumbled. He fell with a thud. Parveen and I hopped up from our seats out of fear. We almost contemplated running on to the field and getting him out of there. But then, we saw he was on his feet again. He began to run.

Parveen and I sat down reluctantly, almost at the edge of the seats.

The other kids were way ahead of him. In a bid to catch up with them, he pushed himself harder. He took a few more steps and then crumbled to the ground again. He fell harder this time. But this time, he got up even quicker. I looked at Parveen and saw that she had tears in her eyes. She pulled down her sunglasses to mask her tears. Because by now, everyone knew about Ayaan's condition and their eyes were on us. I kept a straight face, despite the choking feeling.

Ayaan continued running. The others had completed the race by now. He had just about completed half of. His speed had dropped but he continued to run, taking tiny, sure-footed steps towards the finish line. Everyone watched him with bated breath. As he crossed the finish line, everyone cheered for him. His friends, the parents in the audience, the teachers, the principal and even the other participants. I had started walking towards him from the sidelines to see if he was okay. It was getting too much for me. I was expecting him to look hurt because he didn't win the race. But instead, he turned, searched for me briefly and looked me right in the eye. He winked and flashed me a thumbs-up!

It was too much for me to handle, so I excused myself and walked towards the car. I decided to wait for him back at home, so I turned on the ignition and drove away. I reached home and just dropped myself into the sofa. My mind was numb. I waited for Parveen to bring Ayaan.

He had given all that he had to take on the obstacles that were thrown his way. That was what he taught me in a very simple way. I realized how inadequate I felt when compared to him. There was nothing special about me when this child, after such a traumatic experience, could get up after falling twice, complete the race and then turn around and wink and smile. I learnt a very simple lesson that day. In life, it's all about hanging in there. However much your legs shake, however much you are bruised, you crawl, hop, but get up and take that first step, that's what I learnt from him. After every hurdle I have faced, it's become more clear to me that we need to embrace life with all its tears, screams, the anger, the pain, the shame, because they all demand to be felt. And every time I fall, I have promised myself that however shaky my legs, I will get up. It's only after a disaster that you can resurrect yourself. A little four-year-old has taught me that, the meaning of life.

Soon, Parveen opened the door to our house and he ran up to me. He embraced me tightly and grinned at me. My eyes were beginning to moisten, but I didn't let it go beyond that stage.

'You were so good, Ayaan,' I said. 'I've never seen anyone finish the race so fast despite falling. Everyone's so proud of you! Did you see everyone clapping for you?'

'Papa,' he replied. 'After the race, all my friends were crying because they didn't come first.'

I remained silent as I gazed back into his big, brown eyes.

'But I told them that it's okay,' he continued nonchalantly. 'At least we participated. At least we had fun. Some of my friends even told me that I fell a couple of times and came last. But I told them that I completed the race. Isn't that more important, Papa?'

I didn't know how my little kid had suddenly become so enlightened to be saying these worldly, mature words. I guess the turbulence of the past year had changed his outlook to quite an extent. A year ago, he had cried just like the other kids because he hadn't come first. But now, in his mind he knew that given the circumstances, he had done his best. For me, that was more than any gold medal or first prize. I broke into a smile. I realized that *my son had become Ayaan Man. He was a superhero.*

~

Superheroes have always fascinated me. I remember, as a kid of about seven years, watching Superman and being utterly impressed. When I turned fifteen, I really started to respect and understand all the other superheroes too, as I discovered their backstories. Batman's, for instance, was filled with angst, pain and loss. But he and the other superheroes rose above all the obstacles and become more than just men. They lived with those scars and carried them everywhere they went, without an ounce of self-pity. They turned their weaknesses into strengths.

At nine years of age, I remember telling my father that I didn't want to be just any other man. I wanted to be Superman. He had laughed indulgently, just the way I humour Ayaan now when he says similar things. But fifteen years later, I found myself in films as an actor. In my head, it was almost like being a superhero. I portrayed the roles of ordinary guys in fantastical situations. With age, I realized that being a superhero wasn't always about donning a mask or wearing a cape. It was taking on your hurdles head on and emerging stronger. For me, just like everyone else, life has thrown a fair share of spanners in the wheels of both my personal and professional life.

Bollywood is not an easy place to be in. For all the glitz and glamour it offers, there's also a great deal of murkiness that one has to deal with being a part of this industry. Living in this industry can scar you. But, in that respect, I have built a wall around me. I have isolated my personal and professional life, and the two will seldom intersect. Except for a few people, whom I can count on one hand, I have very few friends in the industry. All my real friends are still my college and school buddies. You wouldn't see me at parties very often and I don't even attend award ceremonies any more. I did perform in a few, very early on in my career, but only because I looked at it as a financial transaction. I have never even dreamt of getting a Filmfare award or any other such felicitation, because I don't seek validation from a statue.

The films that I had worked on while Ayaan was being treated have all released, of course. *Raja Natwarlal, Mr X* and even *Hamari Adhuri Kahani* to a certain extent didn't do as well as I had hoped. Had the entire Ayaan episode not happened, I'm sure I would've been distraught with my dismal run at the box office. But my outlook and mindset have changed. From the happy-go-lucky chap who would shun responsibility during my initial *Footpath* days, I have transformed into a man who can stand up and lock horns with any problem that will be thrown my way. Ayaan's brush with death had resurrected me, so to speak. It has made me the man I was always meant to be. A child has given birth to his father.

I have always held a firm belief that in everyone's life where success or trauma can change you, it's important that you deal with both in a way that is not self-destructive. I was on a high when my films were successful, and then there was this lull when several of my films did not work at the box office back to back. There is a side of the industry that is always ready to write an actor's obituary, writing you off—it is not something new to me. The person who knows me best is myself. You can't have others' opinions about you change the way you look at yourself.

I began to think of myself as a boxer in a ring and my entire career as a long boxing duel. I have had moments where I've given life's hurdles my share of knockout punches. I've also been at the receiving end. Five years ago, I was like the boxer who was at the top of his game. I was invincible. My timing, my form was immaculate. Nobody could fault me. But probably things were going too well. Everything changed in 2014. Life hit me with everything it had. It knocked me down time and again, professionally and personally. What could possibly be worse than hearing that your son has cancer? That's worse than hearing that you have the dreaded disease yourself. So by the time this book will be out, I'll be five film debacles down. Almost written off by bogus opinion makers and scarred with the turbulent battle of my son's cancer. A battle that will go on for another couple of years while he is in remission. But he has made me realize that whatever life throws at you, you endure it. You fight it. Most of the time, life is that formidable opponent in the ring. It will hit you hard. It will pummel you to the ground. But you have to tell yourself to get up, however shaky your legs are. You have to get up each and every single time. And once you do that, you are a champion. A champion who will win the fight. A champion who will taste victory.

Ayaan's cancer was my life's biggest hurdle. Suddenly, I had to prove to myself that I had in me the stuff that my role models were made off. I had to be Superman, in my own little way. I had to not just fight away the enemy that threatened my son's life, but also prove my mettle professionally. And I had to do it together. But the real hero was my son. As I have mentioned earlier, kids like him are made of sterner stuff than we adults are. They battle the disease one day at a time for months, sometimes years, enduring pain and sacrificing their moments of childhood that will never come back. The entire span of his battle for life and the thought of me losing him put my own problems in perspective and made me realize how trivial my problems were.

My son wanted to be Batman. In many ways, he has become him. He has coped with pain and has fought cancer. Just like all stories need a conclusion, the story of Batman needs to end too. I don't have the heart to tell him that Batman doesn't exist. I don't have the strength to tell him that after all those sessions of chemo, he won't have any superpowers. But probably, he will learn by himself, just like I did, that living your life responsibly is a superpower by itself.

So after writing this book, I am going to make one final call to him as Batman. That story needs closure. This time, however, I won't be convincing him to have the meal that he's fussing about or I won't be calming him down before his chemo session. I am going to tell him, 'Son, you have endured it all. You are six years old now, and soon you will finish school and go to college. I will grow old and wither away, and you may have to face the big bad world out there by yourself. But you've got a great head start. You have won the unlikeliest of battles already, so now, whatever it is that comes your way, you have to put on that cape of responsibility, hold your head up high bravely and give all of life's problems that knockout punch.'

EPILOGUE

'Cancer'. A single word that can turn your life upside down. As you may have realized, after Ayaan's diagnosis, I was completely immersed in the research material I had gathered on cancer. Even after his treatment, I kept reading books and articles on the disease. I am obsessed to the point that Parveen thinks I need to see a shrink and get myself cured! But that is what the disease does to you. While going through all the books and articles, I came across some useful things that I think everyone should know. While I have already touched upon some of them in the earlier chapters, I will further elucidate them below as points, so that it is easier for you to understand and use them as reference if need be, especially since a large chunk deals directly with nutrition and natural cancer-battling foods and remedies. It doesn't matter if you are affected with cancer or not, these are some things that everyone ought to know. Because, as the adage goes, 'Prevention is better than cure.'

My mission is to give you information about my discoveries along the way. The standard protocol to fight cancer rarely gives any importance to nutrition. If you eat well and make a few changes to your lifestyle, you have a very high chance of mobilizing the body's resistance to cancer. The point is, you can reverse the cancer and you are the boss. I have come to realize that cancer is a multidimensional disease that can't be cured by a single intervention.

If you mention this to most physicians or anyone associated with the traditional pharma-driven medical world, they will laugh it off and say that there isn't any evidence to back the fact that lifestyle changes can cure cancer. The truth is that changes in lifestyle cannot by definition be patented and so they do not become medications and they therefore can't drive profits for these huge companies. This means that most physicians don't consider lifestyle change as a remedy, and I don't blame them. But it is up to each one of us to make such alterations to our own lives. Also, all great truths go through three phases—first, they are ridiculed, then violently attacked and finally, accepted as self-evident. So read through these points and make an attempt to incorporate them into your everyday lives and you might just end up being healthier than you already are!

- A good nutrition plan leads to prevention of cancer to quite an extent. So it's better to slip into a healthy lifestyle and make the transition smooth, instead of getting the disease first! Because once you're diagnosed with cancer, you have to make a drastic nutritional makeover. You have to bid adieu to all the junk that you've been consuming. The food you have has to be of good quality and natural. You have to start looking out for information like the amount of sugar the food you are about to consume contains, particularly the high-fructose corn syrup variety. What you need to eat are the wholesome foods that nature provides, minus the chemicals and additives. Organically grown fruits and vegetables, whole grains, legumes, beans, nuts, seeds, egg white and select fish need to become part of your nutrition plans. Cancer wasn't as prevalent during the time of our ancestors as it is now. Technology has enabled mass production of food to maximize profits but sadly has also compromised on its essential nutritional value.

- You should adhere to a low glycemic index diet. The glycemic index (GI) is a number associated with a particular type of food that indicates the food's effect on a person's blood sugar level. When we eat foods with a high GI, blood glucose levels shoot up quickly. Studies show that a high GI is associated with cancer of the pancreas, colon and ovaries. Natural sugars—molasses, organic honey, organic jaggery—contain beneficial antioxidants but those, too, should be consumed in moderation.

- Foods like cabbage, apple, carrot, radish, garlic, broccoli, non-GMO soy, ginger, green tea, turmeric, raspberries, blueberries, strawberries and even small amounts of dark chocolate have great anti-cancer effects. Berries, for instance, are very important and rich in flavonoids, which are extremely powerful cancer inhibitors. A moderate quantity of grapes (especially the skin, since it contains a concentrated amount of beneficial compounds) can be a worthy addition to your diet. The juice of grapes, on the other hand, isn't all that good since it has high levels of sugar. Grape and pomegranate seed extracts are useful too. Garlic is effective against leukaemia cells. The fact is that there are so many valuable gifts nature has presented us. It's up to us to use them well!

- Omega-6 oils tend to stimulate excessive proliferation of cancer cells. Omega-3 fats, on the other hand, have exactly the opposite effect and reduce cancer cell multiplication. So take in adequate amount of Omega-3, which is found in flax, walnuts, fish oils, etc. Even your dairy products should be organic, as the cattle they are obtained from are grass-fed, thus the produce is rich in Omega-3, unlike other kinds of dairy products, which are obtained from corn-fed animals.

- Iscador is an extract of the mistletoe plant that has been used for centuries to build up the immune system and fight the growth of cancer cells. In India, homoeopaths have begun to use Iscador for cancer cases. It is manufactured mainly in Switzerland and Germany and is then exported. Just get your doctor to fax a request and order the medicine, and he or she can also instruct you on how to take it.

- Green tea is more beneficial than you think when it comes to cancer. Apart from being extremely fashionable to sip on a cup of green tea, it also has certain molecular switches that can turn off the oncogenes, that is, the genes that have the potential to cause cancer.

- As I mentioned earlier in the chapter, turmeric is extremely helpful in battling cancer cells.

- The option of intravenous Vitamin C is one that should be explored, as it is known to produce high enough blood levels to actually kill cancer cells.

- I don't consume alcohol myself, but if you are someone who likes a drink, I suggest you find your fix in red wine (which contains resveratrol) as it is the only form of alcohol that has some cancer-fighting properties. Also, since we are touching upon bad habits, I request you to please kick the cigarette butt if you are a smoker.

- As much as you can, try to avoid chemicals and pesticides, even those in household products and cosmetics. Baking soda, vinegar, for instance, are good household cleaners. Avoid microwave, and teflon and aluminium foil in cooking ware. Stainless steel, ceramic, glass and iron cooking ware are fine. A number of chemical products are present in our daily environment which help the progression of existing tumours. They include bisphenol A (BPA), which is contained in polycarbonate plastics. For example, reusable plastic bottles, baby bottles, plastic containers with plastic inner linings. When human breast-cancer cells are exposed to BPA, the cells no longer respond to chemotherapy. Similar data has been obtained in studies of food additives which are inorganic phosphate based. So sweetened sodas, processed baked foods and suchlike promote the growth of lung cancers.

- As a species, humans were used to consuming a hundred to three hundred grams of fibre. But now, that's down to a mere fifteen grams. The reason for this is the increase in the levels of consumption of fast food. Fast food and processed foods are known to be without fibre, because they can be frozen and shipped around the world, eaten and cooked faster and have a longer shelf life. So it's absolutely necessary to steer clear of these and get more fibre into your diet.

- Vitamin D stimulates the immune system, and the fact is that in cancer patients the levels of the vitamin are considerably lower than in normal people. It is imperative to address the Vitamin D levels, as it helps support the DNA repairing process. It reduces the risk of cancer development and fights excessive cell proliferation. Sunlight spurs the body to make Vitamin D, which is why you should avoid sunblock, unless you are going to spend hours together in the sun. Salmon, tuna, orange juice, egg yolk are all good sources of Vitamin D. In addition to this, you must also ensure that your levels of Vitamin K are adequate, as it works in tandem with Vitamin D to distribute calcium to the bones. Together, both the vitamins are great for reducing the risk of cancer and also beneficial for the bones, and more importantly, the heart. Vitamin K also reduces the chances of breast cancer in women. Good sources of Vitamin K are dried basil, spinach, broccoli, spring onions and turnip. Selenium supplementation, which has antioxidant properties for breast cancer, can reduce the risk by up to 70 per cent in women. Also, how you metabolize your hormones, and other environmental, lifestyle, hormonal interactions can influence your risk of breast cancer.

- Fasting is a good way of cleaning the body of toxins that have accumulated and for improving the body's waste disposal system. So it is quite smart to rid yourselves of toxins first, if you are suffering from cancer. After that, it would behove you to start with toxin-free food (organic food), to cleanse the tissues and to starve a malignant tumour. It's what chemotherapy does, but in a natural way. Intermittent fasting is recommended for this reason. It is not just a diet or about starving oneself. It is a well-scheduled pattern of eating, so that you can get the most out of your meals.

- As we get older, we are at greater risk of cancer and other diseases that may affect cancer treatment, care and recovery. Ageing is the one big and inevitable risk factor for developing cancer. It also increases the risk of other diseases and injury that can affect a person's well-being, independence, and feelings of self-worth—all issues that need to be considered when cancer treatment decisions are being made, as well as during treatment.

- While reading, I also stumbled upon an interesting bit of information about mammograms that I brought to Parveen's notice immediately. There is evidence that they are not really diagnostic. On the contrary, they can probably even induce breast cancer, especially in highly sensitive women. Women are suggested to undergo a mammogram every year after they turn forty. But the truth is, with the radiation that they are exposed to, if they start out at forty and continue to get one every year till fifty, they would've increased their chances of cancer by a good 30 per cent! The best alternative is to get an MRI scan instead, as it gives much more in terms of a diagnostic picture. The clearest vision of the breast is with an

MRI scan. A thermogram is also a good alternative, as a tumour is hot, and will pop up in the scan. Women without children, or who have their first pregnancy after the age of thirty, have a slightly higher risk of developing breast cancer than those who become pregnant while they are younger. Breastfeeding may also reduce the risk of breast cancer slightly.

- All men over the age of forty-five should get their PSA levels checked regularly. Any abnormality in the levels might lead to prostate cancer.

- A biopsy is a process where a tissue sample from a tumour is taken by a surgeon, and analysed under the microscope to check for the presence of cancer. A positive biopsy report typically involves immediate treatment via surgery, chemo or radiation. Biopsies are potentially dangerous because puncturing the tumour can release microscopic quantities of cancer cells into the surrounding lymphatic system of blood vessels. This can allow the cancer cells to move to distant organs and grow. This is not always the case and it won't metastasize every time, but there is a possibility. Sometimes, a mere blood test gives enough information to determine how your immunity function is performing and can indicate a cancer, before you actually move towards taking more serious tests. Some screening procedures can cause bleeding or other problems. For example, colon cancer screening with colonoscopy can cause tears in the lining of the colon. Also, both false positive and false negative results are possible. This is the reason why it is advisable to always get a second opinion.

- Nearly all cases of cervical cancer are caused by infection with oncogenic, or high-risk, types of human papillomavirus, or HPV. Although HPV infection is very common, most infections will be suppressed by the immune system within a year or two without causing cancer. Cervical cancer screening is a vital part of a woman's routine health care. Cervical cancer screening includes two types of screening tests: cytology-based screening, known as the Pap test or Pap Smear, and HPV testing. The main purpose of screening with the Pap test is to detect abnormal cells that may develop into cancer if left untreated. The Pap test can also find non-cancerous conditions, such as infections and inflammation. It can also find cancer cells. In regularly screened populations, however, the Pap test identifies most abnormal cells before they become cancer. So it is necessary to get a Pap Smear test done.

The number of global cancer deaths by 2030 is estimated to be a whopping 11.5 million! But interestingly, 40 per cent of cancer deaths can be prevented. More than 50 per cent of all cancers occur in developing countries. And with the way our country is getting Westernized, especially in the sense of dietary changes, cancer getting out of hand is a scary but inevitable prospect. India has some of the world's highest incidences of cancer—cervical, gall bladder, oral and pharynx According to the World Health Organization, lung, oral, lip, throat and neck cancers are the most common among men while women suffer more from cervix, breast and ovarian cancers. High treatment costs are one of the main reasons why cancer care is out of reach for millions of Indians. If detected early, treatment is effective and cheaper. But, if detected late, it is more expensive and also reduces the chances of survival.

I read an interesting article on the *India Today* website that broke up the cancer-affected regions in India regionally. Which goes as follows: in the North-east, the cancer rates are relatively higher than in other regions of India, especially of the oesophagus. West Bengal has high rates of lung and urinary bladder cancer. South and coastal regions have high rates of stomach cancer, as their diet is rich in spices and salts. Goa has a lot of colon cancer patients, since they consume a lot of red meat, alcohol and tobacco. Gujarat and Rajasthan have high rates of head and neck cancer because of tobacco and pan masala consumption. Madhya Pradesh also has the most cases of oral cancers, tobacco and pan masala being the main culprits. All cancers are higher than average in Punjab, especially kidney, urinary bladder and breast cancers because of pollution, pesticides and toxins in food. The other problem in India is the lack of awareness. For example, people are not entirely aware of the risks of smoking. But then, even those who know of the downfalls continue to consume carcinogenic products. It's dangerous to have this bogus belief that you're invincible. With the repeated usage of these contaminants and carcinogens, your body will break down. You will start developing other diseases, apart from cancer, like type-2 diabetes and heart diseases.

I have friends and acquaintances who continue to let their kids indulge in processed, canned, packaged, refined foods, sodas, etc. and they stubbornly shoot down any advice on changing their lifestyle and dietary habits. Their justification is that the whole world is doing it. Well my plea to them and other parents is that, with all the knowledge available, you by all means have the freedom to continue these suicidal habits, but for God's sake, don't impose them on your kids because unlike you, they don't know that they have a choice. You make that choice for them. It's better to have them dislike you now for a while because you deprived them of an unhealthy lifestyle than have them curse you later on, once the consequences raise their ugly head.

Cancer is now one of the top causes of death in India. It is time for all of you to take note and do what you can to fight it. Now that I do know more than the layman about cancer, I felt that it was my responsibility to put forth whatever I had studied and learned from various sources (doctors, books, articles, etc.) during the entire phase of Ayaan's treatment, in a concise manner.

ACKNOWLEDGEMENTS

This book wouldn't have been in your hands had I not had the support and help of certain people in my life. So I would like to thank them all. Starting with my family, I want to thank my wife—Parveen. She has been a pillar of strength through the entire episode. She is an amazing woman who has braved all the hurdles with an air of optimism and hope. It was her and my son's resilience and endurance that inspired me and eventually pushed me to write this book. I thank my parents, my mother-in-law and my brother-in-law Avinash, for being there for us whenever we needed them emotionally. All the time they gave, helped Ayaan towards his speedy recovery. A special mention to Avi, who always prioritized Ayaan's visits to the hospital over his work.

Thank you Smiley Suri for being so supportive through the treatment and spending countless hours at the hospital. Thank you Bhatt Sahaab, for being there with me through those horrific six months of treatment. You were always there when I needed to talk or vent. Thanks Kum Kum Saigal, my chotumasi, for being there at the hospital every day. Thanks to Dr Uma for all the visits she made to Hinduja when Ayaan was being operated and also for checking up on him from time to time.

Parveen and I want to thank our friends and the rest of our families for standing by us during this most testing phase of our life. You were all there when we needed you emotionally and helped us do our research, like finding out treatment options, or even just being there to talk to whenever we felt low. Thanks Akshay Kumar, for always checking up if we needed your help in Toronto. A thank you to all the other people from the film fraternity who called in to check up on Ayaan's health. Thanks Yuvraj Singh for the invaluable advice.

Thank you Dr Banavali from Tata Memorial Hospital and all of Ayaan's paediatric doctors—Dr Ajit Gajendragadkar, Dr Abha Gupta, Dr Jill, the staff at Hinduja Hospital, and everyone at SickKids Hospital. Thanks to Luke Coutinho, the world renowned nutritionist, for his useful suggestions on eating right. A thank you to all the doctors that I called and pestered on a daily basis, to find out different treatment options and information on Ayaan's cancer.

A special mention for the person who nudged me to write this book, S. Hussain Zaidi. I remember the day he informally visited me on the sets to narrate a story and we got talking about my son's health, who at that time was still undergoing his treatment in Canada. I told him about the entire incident and also mentioned the steps we were taking to make sure he had a speedy recovery. Hussain said, 'The memory of the incident is so fresh and clear in your mind that you should pen it down. You should write a book. It will be something your son can grow up and read and he will be proud of himself. With time, memories fade. Like great memories, painful ones need to be held close too. Because it is testament to your resilience, something you and your family could endure.'

Thank you Bilal Siddiqi, for writing the book with me. He's the one who nudged me on a regular basis and pushed me to dig deeper and recall all the events in detail. Hussain and Bilal made me relive incidences from my early years in the film industry, giving the book a fabulous structure. Thank you, Bilal, for your patience.

Thank you Milee Ashwarya, and the entire team at Penguin for supporting this book and making sure it reaches out to all the families who are victims of this dreaded disease and are in search of hope. Thank you Rohan Shrestha, for the photos you clicked for the cover of the book.

And finally, but most importantly, a big thank you to all my fans for their prayers and best wishes. The entire nation and so many people in Canada prayed for Ayaan when they heard the news. I received fan mails from different countries, usually from Indians, who had read about it and were so moved by the incident. I can't thank you all enough for all your prayers. They have paid off.